CRÉ
1346

The church of St Martin in Picquigny. (Peter Hoskins)

CRÉCY 1346

*A Tourist's Guide to the Campaign
by Car, by Bike and on Foot*

Peter Hoskins
with Richard Barber

Pen & Sword
MILITARY

First published in Great Britain in 2016 by
PEN & SWORD MILITARY
an imprint of
Pen & Sword Books Ltd
47 Church Street
Barnsley
South Yorkshire
S70 2AS

ISBN 978 147382 701 1

A CIP catalogue record for this book is
available from the British Library.

Typeset in Palatino and Optima by
CHIC GRAPHICS

Printed in India by Replika Press Pvt. Ltd.

Pen & Sword Books Ltd incorporates the imprints of
Pen & Sword Archaeology, Atlas, Aviation, Battleground, Discovery,
Family History, History, Maritime, Military, Naval, Politics, Railways,
Select, Social History, Transport, True Crime, Claymore Press,
Frontline Books, Leo Cooper, Praetorian Press, Remember When,
Seaforth Publishing and Wharncliffe.

For a complete list of Pen & Sword titles please contact
PEN & SWORD BOOKS LTD
47 Church Street, Barnsley, South Yorkshire, S70 2AS, England
E-mail: enquiries@pen-and-sword.co.uk
Website: www.pen-and-sword.co.uk

CONTENTS

PREFACE

The origins of this guide lie in my project, which I started in 2005, to follow on foot the campaigns of the Black Prince leading to his victory over King John II of France at the Battle of Poitiers in 1356. The aim was to bring a fresh look to the campaigns of 1355 and 1356 by supplementing more conventional historical research with exploration on the ground. Some readers found the book that followed, *In the Steps of the Black Prince, The Road to Poitiers 1355–1356*, useful and interesting when touring near the routes of the Black Prince's campaigns, even though it lacked both detailed information on routes and practical information for tourists. Although it was not intended as a guide book, it was evident that the story and the places which featured in *In the Steps of the Black Prince* provided the elements for interesting holidays or excursions for those with an interest in history.

With the approach of the 600th anniversary of the Battle of Agincourt it seemed, based on my experience with *In the Steps of the Black Prince,* that there was room for a book specifically written to help the historical tourist follow the campaign. Thus, *Agincourt 1415: A Tourist's Guide to the Campaign* followed. The next logical step was to write a similar guide for that great precursor to Agincourt: Crécy. This book takes the tourist from the landing place for Edward III and his army at St-Vaast-la-Hougue, through the battlefield near the village of Crécy-en-Ponthieu to Calais, where Edward settled down to besiege and capture the town.

The guide tells the story of the campaign, drawing on my experience walking the route of the English march. For the history I have drawn extensively on Richard Barber's work, particularly his *Edward III and the Triumph of England,* as well as local histories. This guide book follows Edward III's route in Galfridi Le Baker de Swynebroke, *Chronicon*, edited by E.M. Thompson. A modern and more easily obtained version of this valuable chronicle is *The Chronicle of Geoffrey Le Baker of Swinbrook* by Richard Barber translated by David

Preest. This book is not intended to be an analytical history of the campaign, and it does not, therefore, either discuss in depth some of the uncertainties associated with the battle and Edward's march, or attempt to analyse and interpret the varying accounts in the primary sources. Where there is such uncertainty I have opted for what seems to me to be the most probable interpretation. The choices are mine.

For those who would like authoritative detail and analysis of the battle, they can do no better than read Richard Barber's *Edward III and the Triumph of England*. This book also argues strongly for the crossing of the Somme having been closer to the river estuary than others have assumed. The *Battle of Crécy, 1346* by Andrew Ayton and Sir Philip Preston is a valuable source for the reader who wishes to read the story of this battle in depth. The chapter by Sir Philip Preston which discusses the traditional site of the battlefield is particularly useful. Some recently published work by Kelly de Vries and Michael Livingstone in *The Battle of Crécy, A Casebook* suggests an alternative site for the battle.

Peter Hoskins

ACKNOWLEDGEMENTS

I am particularly grateful to Richard Barber for his contribution to this book. I could never expect to match his knowledge of King Edward III, his eldest son Edward the Black Prince and the period in which they lived, and I was, therefore, delighted when he agreed to allow me to draw on his published work and also to advise me on the text. He has given a good deal of his time and patience to advising me and I cannot thank him enough for his guidance.

I am also grateful to my walking companions John Griffin, Martin Hoskins, and David Finnimore, who patiently followed parts of the route with me. My thanks also to those who have allowed me to use their photographs and illustrations: Richard Barber, Paul Hitchen and Chris Dawson. Finally, and by no means least, thanks to Scott Hall for the time and skill he has devoted to drawing the maps and the plan of Caen.

ADVICE FOR TOURISTS

Introduction
This guide has been written primarily with the motorist in mind, but with additional information for those who want to follow the routes either on foot or on a touring bicycle. The guide is divided into six tours following the itinerary of Edward III and his army from the landing at St-Vaast-la-Hougue, through the battlefield at Crécy-en-Ponthieu, to Calais, where Edward III settled down to besiege and capture the town. Five tours cover the route from St-Vaast-la-Hougue to Calais and the sixth covers the battlefield. A half-day visit will allow ample time to see the battlefield and the museum in the village of Crécy-en-Ponthieu. The other tours can each be covered in a day or so by car. Two or three days would be comfortable for a cyclist, and the walker will need to allow about a week for each tour. Walking the entire route would require about five weeks.

How to Get There and Back by Public Transport
The tours start and finish at towns of sufficient size to provide a selection of accommodation. The nearest airports for each tour are given, and with the walker and cyclist in mind there is information on rail access to the start and end of each tour. Information is also given on intermediate towns with access by public transport to enable walkers and cyclists to tailor tours to meet time available or particular interests.

The French railways, *SNCF*, have an extensive network. They also run co-ordinated bus, *autocar* or *car* services as replacements for defunct lines to link some rail services. The website for planning a journey is www.voyages-sncf.com. An English language version, www. voyages-sncf.co.uk, will take you to Rail Europe, www.raileurope. co.uk. These sites will generally give you all the information you need for the route. However, the network is organized regionally and full timetables, details on station services and locations, and route maps are given on regional websites. Start on www.ter-sncf.com and then go to the appropriate region: Haute-Normandie, Picardie and Nord-Pas-de-Calais. For rail journeys in the Île-de-France use www.transilien.com. Tickets for trains on the Île-de-France services cannot be booked in advance.

Eurolines, www.eurolines.fr, operate a number of long-distance bus routes in France. However, there is no equivalent to National Express in the UK, and finding details of local bus services can be time consuming. A good starting point will often be the website for the prefecture of the *département* in question. Some towns also have websites which give information about bus and coach services. Many rural bus services are geared to getting people to and from work and children to and from school, so there are often services early in the morning, around midday and in the evening, with little or nothing in the way of services in between.

For those walkers and cyclists travelling to and from the tours by car, parking is available at *SNCF* stations at the start and finish of each route and at intermediate points. Outside of major towns parking at stations is generally free. In addition, it is usually possible to find other parking free of charge in small towns and villages. However, some car parks double as market-places, and when parking it is advisable to check that there is not a parking prohibition on market days. This will normally be indicated on a sign nearby. French railways are relatively bicycle-friendly, and it is usually possible to take a bicycle, *vélo*, on the train: www.velo.sncf.com. Cyclists should check before planning a tour, but there is not normally a charge for taking cycles on regional trains, *TER*. Similarly, carriage on some Intercity trains, *IC*, is free, but sometimes a reservation is required and in that case a charge is levied. Capacity on high-speed trains, *TGV*, is limited, reservation is mandatory and invariably a charge will be made. Carriages in which bicycles can be loaded are generally marked with a large bicycle symbol on the window, and in some trains easy to use hanging racks are provided. Bicycles cannot generally be taken on buses, but some buses operated by *SNCF* do carry cycles. Information on cycle carriage on *SNCF* operated buses can be found on the route timetable, *fiche horaire*, on regional websites. The *SNCF* journey planner on the main French site, www.voyages-sncf.com, also indicates services on which bicycles can be carried with standard symbols. This site also indicates when disabled access is available on a service.

Where to Stay

In view of the dynamic nature of the accommodation market, and differing personal preferences for where to stay and daily travelling distances, I have not given specific information on hotels and bed and breakfast establishments. However, there is a wide range of up-to-date information available on the Internet with a number of excellent websites to help in the search for accommodation. For bed and breakfast *Gîtes de France*, www.gites-de-france.com, *Clévacances*, www.clevacances.com, and *Airbnb*, www.airbnb.com, are good starting points. *Logis*, www.logishotels.com, provides information on a wide range of independent hotels. All these websites have an interactive map search facility with an option for use in English, and *Gîtes de France*, *Clévacances* and *Logis* all publish printed guides. Yellow Pages, *Pages Jaunes*, www.pagesjaunes.fr, can also be useful and results are shown on maps. There is also a useful smart phone application for *Pages Jaunes*. Tourist office, *office* or *bureau de tourisme*, and town websites also often give details of accommodation, *hébergement*. A list of the more important tourist offices is given for each tour.

Finding accommodation can be particularly problematic for the walker, who cannot deviate significant distances from the route to find a bed and breakfast or hotel. If the tourist websites do not bring results, then a general Internet search for *chambre d'hôte* at the planned destination may do so. All *chambres d'hôte* are required to register with their local *mairie*, the municipal office in each town or village. A call to the *mairie*, which can be found through *Pages Jaunes*, may throw up something not available through other sources. This may need some persistence, since in small villages the *mairie* will often not be open throughout the week. Another avenue is to post a notice on either the Normandy or Picardy & Nord-Pas-de-Calais regional websites of Anglo Info France, a network for expatriates: http://france.angloinfo. com.

Municipal and private campsites are numerous in France, but many have a short season. Town and tourist office websites are again useful sources of information for campers. A further source is: www.campingfrance.com/UK/. Camping in the wild, *camping sauvage*, may seem attractive in a large country such as France. However, there are restrictions on camping away from established sites, particularly in forests and national or regional natural parks. Details on regulations and some recommended sites can be found at http://Le-camping-sauvage.fr.

walkers. Variations for cyclists from the routes on foot are given only where the walking routes may be unsuitable for cycling. A road atlas may suffice for cyclists if they are happy to keep to numbered roads. However, the cyclist who wishes to get away from main roads will require more detailed maps. The *IGN* publishes a selection of maps at 1:100,000 (*Cartes Tourisme et Découverte: TOP 100*), as well as the 1:25,000 (*Série Bleu*). In the past the *IGN* also published a series of maps at 1:50,000 (*Série Orange*). Some maps in this series are still available from the *IGN*, but stocks are not being replaced as they become exhausted. In addition, those that do remain have not been updated for some years. In view of these difficulties references for 1:50,000 scale maps are not given, but those at 1:25,000 and 1:100,000 are listed for each tour. Maps published by the *IGN* can be obtained from www.ign.fr or suppliers in the United Kingdom such as Stanford Travel: http://travel.stanfords. co.uk/.

I have not divided walking and cycling routes into daily sections, since everyone will have their own preferences for pace and distance. The route descriptions were accurate at the time of writing, but things do change as new roads are constructed and paths come and go. Walkers and cyclists should check that they have the latest edition of maps and be prepared to adapt to changes when they are on tour.

Walking and Cycling in France

A marked difference between the UK and France for walkers and cyclists is that there are no rights of way on paths in the sense that we understand them in Great Britain. In addition, tracks come and go. Just because a track is on the map does not mean it is on the ground, and just because a track is on the ground does not mean it is on the map. Sometimes what looks like a good track or minor road on the map just disappears into a field, or a house has been built across it surrounded by a long impenetrable fence. I have on occasion struck off across fields on a compass bearing to intercept a road rather than retrace my steps. Fortunately, French farmers are generally relaxed about property rights and seem to think nothing of a walker trudging across their land in search of the path, and of course the French are generally very well disposed towards cyclists.

France is blessed with an extensive network of way-marked footpaths. Many of these are organized locally, but others come under the auspices of the French walking association *Fédération Française de la Randonnée*: www.ffrandonnee.fr. National long-distance paths are known as *Sentiers de Grande Randonnée*, and given a number prefixed *GR* (e.g. *GR353*); they are way-marked in red and white. Horizontal red and white bars mark the route, a red and white cross means 'not this way', and red and white arrows set at right angles indicate turns. Regional routes are known as *Sentiers de Grande Randonnée du Pays* (*GRP*). These routes are way-marked in a similar way in red and yellow. *GR* and *GRP* paths are usually marked on recent editions of 1:25,000 maps. Local routes which are generally of short distance and aimed more at the rambler out for the day are known as *Sentiers de Promenade et Randonnée* (*PR*); they are way-marked in yellow. On occasions the tours in the guide follow designated paths for short distances and the way-marking can be useful.

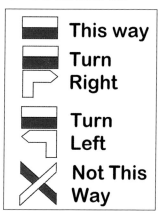

Many forests in France are open to the public and provide long pleasant walks, often in ancient oak woods, but occasionally forest areas are private and are fenced off for hunting – *chasse privé* or *chasse gardé*. Furthermore, hunting in public areas in France, in the sense of shooting of deer and boar, *sanglier*, with rifles is widespread in the hunting season. The dates for the hunting season vary from region to region, but typically the season runs from late August or early September to the beginning of March. The season can be longer in fenced-off parks or forests. In public areas roads where hunting is in progress will be marked with signs such as *chasse en cours*.

Conventional footpath signs – red and white for long-distance paths (GR) and red and yellow for regional paths (GRP), but frequently used in different colours for other paths.

The hunters themselves will be wearing fluorescent jackets and will take every precaution to respect walkers, but it would be foolhardy to go off the main tracks in woods where hunting is under way. Apart from the risks due to the hunting itself, crossing the path of a boar being pursued by hounds is not to be recommended. In normal circumstances these magnificent beasts are most unlikely to pose a threat, but they are wild animals and they can be aggressive either to defend their young or if they feel threatened.

Boar are very numerous in France, and hunting is regulated to maintain a stable population: around half a million boar are killed every year to achieve this. Despite this, although I have often seen signs of their presence, I have only once seen boar during my walks of more than 4,000km in France and that was in the Forêt de Crécy.

As a final point, I advise walkers to carry a compass. This may seem unnecessary for this kind of walking, but I have frequently found it useful to resolve a route ambiguity, to walk where a track has disappeared and even to find the way out of a town!

Safety

The routes described in this guide are neither remote nor in the 'big outdoors'. Nonetheless, some sections of the walks are on paths away from roads or in forests that are used infrequently. In addition, mobile telephone coverage is by no means comprehensive. A minor accident in such circumstances can become hazardous, and it is prudent to take some basic safety precautions. I always carry a survival bag and a whistle to attract attention. I also always leave an itinerary with someone, giving start and stop points and accommodation planned for each day. If I am walking alone, I invariably telephone each evening the person who holds the itinerary to confirm my safe arrival.

France is less densely populated than the United Kingdom, and cycling and walking can be a great pleasure. Nevertheless, walking or cycling on roads is not without risk and some simple precautions should be taken. The French highway code, *Code de la Route*, requires pedestrians to use footpaths alongside the roads when provided, rather than walking on the road. When there are no paths, then the pedestrian must walk on the left-hand side of the road unless this presents a hazard to them. Pedestrians and cyclists are also strongly advised to wear high-visibility clothing or tabards; this is particularly important in poor visibility. Other than on the quietest of roads walkers are also well advised to walk in single file.

What Happened

There is an introductory chapter, Edward III and the Hundred Years War, to put the story of the Crécy campaign within its historical context. Each tour also has a description of events relevant to the route followed.

What to See

The tours go through areas which suffered extensive damage during the First and Second World Wars. In the First World War some villages were totally obliterated, and had to be rebuilt completely. Similarly, in Normandy many towns and villages were destroyed or severely damaged during the Battle of Normandy in 1944. Much of the rich medieval heritage of this part of France was destroyed, but some survived and some was painstakingly restored. For each tour places to visit are recommended and numbered in the narrative of events, the route descriptions and on the maps. These places are those of historical interest linked to the story of the campaign which generally have buildings with at least elements which have either survived from the time of Edward III's campaign or have been faithfully restored. Directions to places of interest away from the main route are given for the motorist, but the walking and cycling tours only take in the principal places along the main route. GPS co-ordinates are given for places to visit. The co-ordinates are in decimal form, but there are numerous conversion websites available if degrees, minutes and seconds of latitude and longitude are preferred.

EDWARD III AND THE HUNDRED YEARS WAR

Edward III's great victory at Crécy-en-Ponthieu in 1346 sent shock waves throughout Europe. There had been earlier English victories since the start of the war with France, now known as the Hundred Years War, nine years earlier. However, this victory marked the start of a period when the English seemed invincible. Ten years later there was a further great victory at Poitiers. The subsequent Treaty of Brétigny in 1360 ceded large areas of France to the English crown and seemed set to deliver Edward III a long-term peace with France. Edward III's achievements, including his victory at Crécy, have earned him a reputation as one of the greatest of English kings. However, Crécy is often viewed in isolation from the broader history of the Hundred Years War. His success can be better appreciated by looking at it within the context of the war as a whole.

Causes of the Hundred Years War

There were two underlying causes of the war which started in 1337: the homage claimed by the French kings from the kings of England for their lands in France, and the English claim to the throne of France. They remained central to the conflict between England and France throughout the war.

The anomaly whereby English kings owed homage to kings of France can be traced back to William the Conqueror, who was both King William I of England and Duke of Normandy. The situation was exacerbated when Henry II came to the throne in 1154. He had acquired extensive lands in south-western France through his marriage to Eleanor of Aquitaine. Thus, he and subsequent English kings ruled the Duchy of Aquitaine centred on the city of Bordeaux. The status of Aquitaine was a persistent cause of dispute between the kings of England and France over the years, with kings of France demanding homage from the English kings who proclaimed their right to full sovereignty as Duke of Aquitaine. In the years immediately preceding the Hundred Years War there were protracted diplomatic wrangles between Edward III and Philip VI. Matters came to a head in 1337 with a dispute over the extradition from England of a French exile, Robert of Artois, a one-time adviser to Philip. Edward refused to return Robert to France, and Philip declared Edward's Duchy of Aquitaine forfeit. With war coming, Edward revoked his homage for Aquitaine.

The issue of homage for Aquitaine should have been resolved by the Treaty of Brétigny of 1360 between Edward III and John II of France after the English victory at Poitiers in 1356. Under a protocol associated with the treaty Edward III agreed to renounce his claim to the throne of France in return for French agreement that he should hold Aquitaine in full sovereignty. Unfortunately, King John II died in 1364 before these terms were put into effect, and the issue remained in the forefront of the quarrel between England and France. In 1369 Charles V reclaimed sovereignty over Aquitaine and Edward III took up the title of King of France once more. In 1399, on his father's accession as Henry IV, the thirteen-year-old future Henry V was named Duke of Aquitaine, but the dispute over sovereignty came into sharp focus again in early 1401 when the French king, as a deliberate slight to Henry IV, named the Dauphin Louis, his eldest son and hence heir to the throne, Duke of Guienne (the French name for Aquitaine). The importance of resolving the dispute over sovereignty for Aquitaine was not lost on the young Henry, and it was a central tenet of his policy towards France after his accession as King Henry V in 1413.

The second cause of the war was the claim of English kings to the crown of France. On the death of the French King Charles IV in 1328 the closest male successor was Edward III of England through his mother Isabella, sister to Charles IV and daughter of Philip IV.

The crux of the matter was whether the crown could be passed through the female line. The French view was that a woman could not inherit the crown and that she could not, therefore, pass this right to her son. Thus, Philip, the next closest male successor, who could trace his lineage back to Philip III through an unbroken male line, assumed the title of King Philip VI – the first of the Valois dynasty. There was a somewhat desultory attempt by the English to lay claim to the throne

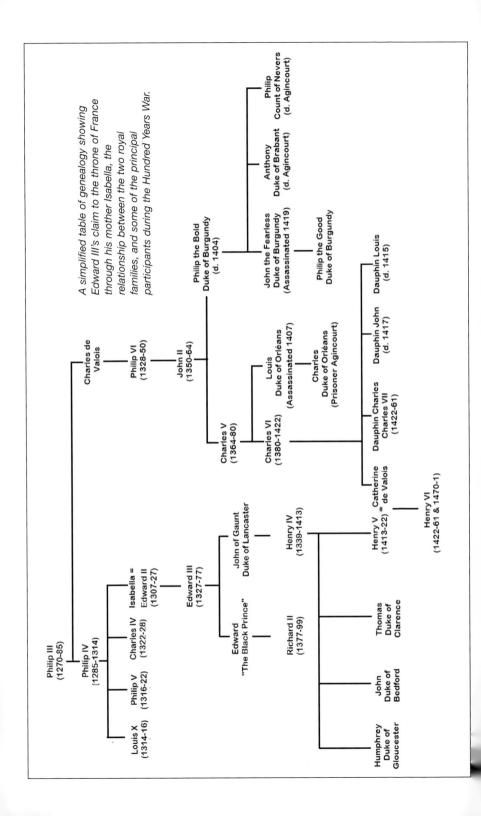

A simplified table of genealogy showing Edward III's claim to the throne of France through his mother Isabella, the relationship between the two royal families, and some of the principal participants during the Hundred Years War.

on behalf of the fifteen-year-old Edward III. This received short shrift in France, and there the matter lay until the third year of the war in 1340 when Edward formally laid claim to the crown of France.

It is not clear whether or not Edward held this claim as a serious war aim. Since, in the Treaty of Brétigny, he was prepared to trade the claim to the throne for sovereignty over Aquitaine, it may have been simply a way of encouraging allies and exerting negotiating pressure on Philip VI and his successor John II. With the failure to implement the treaty the issue remained unresolved throughout the rest of Edward III's life and the remainder of the war.

The Outbreak of War and the English Ascendancy, 1337–1360
First Moves
In May 1337 Philip VI's decision that the Duchy of Aquitaine should be forfeit due to Edward III's refusal to deliver Robert of Artois, who had been accused of forgery, into the hands of the French led to Edward's revocation of homage. Philip had already proclaimed the *arrière-ban* to summon a royal army, and the war which was to span the reigns of five French and five English kings and known to us now as the Hundred Years War had been unleashed.

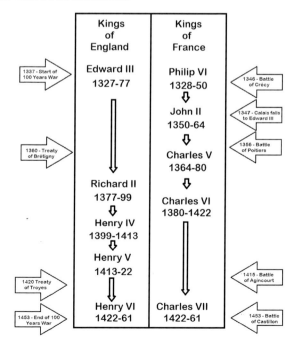

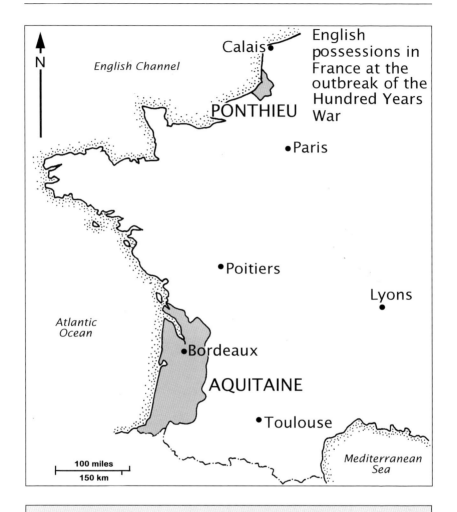

English possessions in France at the outbreak of the Hundred Years War

The Protagonists

King Edward III

Edward III, born at Windsor in 1312, was one of the greatest English monarchs. The reign of his father, Edward II, was a disaster, marked in particular by the defeat of an English army by the Scots at Bannockburn in 1315. With Edward II's reign going from bad to worse, the young Prince Edward's mother, Queen Isabella, in conspiracy with her lover Roger Mortimer, deposed Edward II in the name of her son in 1327. Isabella and Mortimer were *de facto* rulers until, shortly before his eighteenth birthday, Edward seized power in a daring coup at

Nottingham castle in 1330 assisted by amongst others William Montagu, later Earl of Salisbury. Edward III is perhaps best known for his great victory at Crécy and for the foundation of the Order of the Garter in 1349. His victory at Crécy, and the Black Prince's subsequent victory at Poitiers in 1356, was based on fundamental strategic and tactical innovations developed in the earlier years of his reign in fighting in Scotland. At the strategic level, Edward recognized that England must carry the war to France to counter the greater wealth and manpower of his adversary. A key element of this strategy was the *chevauchée*, a highly mobile raid deep into enemy territory with the objectives of encouraging friends, punishing enemies and, where possible, bringing the French to battle on favourable terms. Tactically, Edward's approach was to select a strong defensive position and coax his enemy to attack his dismounted men-at-arms and archers arrayed

to optimize the impact of their shooting. The success of these strategic and tactical changes was such that the reputation of English arms was completely overturned during his reign, to the point that an Italian commentator, the poet and scholar Petrarch, said after the Battle of Poitiers: 'In my youth, those Britons called English were taken as the most timid of barbarians. Today they are a very bellicose people. They have beaten the ancient military glory of France, in victories so numerous and unheard of that these people formerly inferior to the wretched Scots, in addition to the deplorable catastrophe of a great king that I cannot recall without sighing, have crushed the realm by fire and steel, and are barely recognizable.' Edward was also instrumental in

An artist's impression of King Edward III. (Paul Hitchen)

making far-reaching and enduring changes in the administrative and legislative fields, not least in introducing English as the language of the courts and parliament in 1360. He came close to achieving his war aims with the Treaty of Brétigny in 1360. However, the failure of Edward and John II of France to ratify the protocols relating to sovereignty and the renunciation of Edward's claim to the throne of France led, after John's death in 1364, to the unravelling of all the English gains with a return to war in the latter years of his reign.

Edward of Woodstock, the Black Prince
Edward of Woodstock, named after his birthplace at the palace of Woodstock near Oxford where Blenheim Palace now stands, was the eldest son of King Edward III and Queen Philippa. He was created Earl of Chester in 1333, became as Duke of Cornwall from 1337 the first English Duke, was invested as Prince of Wales from 1343 and served as Prince of Aquitaine from 1362 to 1372. He was one of the most remarkable men of his time, and, although there are no contemporary records of his nickname, he later became widely known as the Black Prince in England and France. Born on 15 June 1330, he was barely sixteen years of age at the battle of Crécy and yet he fought with distinction in the thick of the combat. At a time when set-piece battles were rare and risky events he went on to gain great victories at Poitiers in 1356 and Nájera in Spain in 1367. His victory at Poitiers in 1356 was, with the rout of the French army and the capture of King John II, his greatest triumph, giving his father the best opportunity of his reign to bring the war to a successful conclusion. Nájera, fought by rival claimants to the throne of Castile, in effect a proxy battle between France and England when the two countries were supposed to be at peace, proved to be something of a Pyrrhic victory for the prince. His protégé, Pedro the Cruel, reneged on his promise to finance the campaign, and as a consequence the prince imposed unpopular taxes on his subjects in Aquitaine which were to contribute to the collapse of the peace of Brétigny in 1370. In addition, he contracted an illness while in Spain, possibly amoebic dysentery, which became increasingly debilitating and led to his death in 1376, shortly before his forty-sixth birthday. Most unusually for an heir to the throne he married Joan Holland, the Fair Maid of Kent, for love rather than dynastic reasons. He had two sons, the first of whom, Edward of Angoulême, died at five

An artist's impression of Edward of Woodstock, Prince of Wales, now commonly known as the Black Prince. Just visible is the white label of cadency, a horizontal bar with three downward points. This label differentiates the prince's arms from those of his father and shows that he is the eldest son. (Paul Hitchen)

years of age in 1370. The prince predeceased his father by a year, leaving his younger son, Richard of Bordeaux, to succeed Edward III as the unfortunate King Richard II in 1377. The regard in which the prince was held by contemporaries was reflected in the service of commemoration held by King Charles V of France, despite the two countries being once again at war.

King Philip VI

When Philip de Valois was born in 1293 his uncle Philip IV was on the French throne. The possibility that the days of the Capetian dynasty were numbered and that Philip would one day accede to the throne would have seemed remote. However, the death of Philip IV in 1314 was followed by a series of short reigns by his sons Louis X (1314–1316), Philip V (1316–1322) and Charles IV (1322–1328). When Charles died without issue, Philip de Valois became one of two claimants. Edward III of England had the most direct claim as grandson of Philip IV through his mother, while Philip's claim was as the eldest grandson of Philip III. Philip's trump was that his line of succession was entirely male. In French eyes he also had the advantage of being French and thirty-five years old, a much better prospect than the fifteen-year-old English Prince Edward, still very much under the control of his

mother and Roger Mortimer. A council of magnates, the twelve peers of France, chose Philip as king. He succeeded Charles as Philip VI, the first of a Valois dynasty which was to rule France until 1589. His relationship with Edward III was one of personal enmity, with Edward addressing him as 'you who call yourself King of France', a form he did not use with Philip's successors. Philip's accession, based as it was on the support of the leading members of the nobility, left him more constrained in his ability to impose his will than he might have been had he taken the throne as a straightforward hereditary right. He was an experienced soldier, and in general his approach to battle was cautious, choosing to

An artist's impression of Philip de Valois, King Philip VI of France. (Paul Hitchen)

avoid attacks against his opponents in strong defensive positions. His attack on the English at Crécy was entirely out of character, and probably resulted more from events running away from him rather than a conscious decision. He won an important battle against the Flemish at Cassel in 1328, but this success was overshadowed by French defeats at the hands of the English at Sluys and Crécy, and by his failure to bring Edward III to battle in Flanders in 1338 or to relieve the siege of Calais in 1347. On the diplomatic front he was a worthy adversary for Edward, but he lacked the flair and charisma of Edward, did not get on well with the senior French nobility, and was plagued throughout his reign by problems of maintaining the loyalty and unity of his subjects. On his death in 1350 he was succeeded by his son John, Duke of Normandy, who as John II was defeated and captured at Poitiers by the Black Prince.

At the start of the war both kings expected that Aquitaine and the south-west of France would be the principal theatre of operations and planned to lead their armies there personally. Indeed, in the first years of the war there were some French incursions into Aquitaine, where a small number of English reinforcements had been despatched. Also there was some cross-channel raiding by both sides, but as events unfolded it became apparent to the English and the French that the main focus would be to the north and neither king went to the south-west.

In the north attention turned to the Low Countries, where there was widespread discontent with relationships with France. Edward III sought to exploit Philip's difficulties by forging an alliance with Louis of Bavaria, the Emperor of the Holy Roman Empire, and discontented lords in the Low Countries. Edward landed at Antwerp in July 1338 and made his way to Coblenz. Here he was appointed the Emperor's vicar, effectively vice-regent, in Western Europe for seven years and the Emperor's nobles gave Edward their homage. Edward summoned the nobles of the region to join his army in July 1339 with the objective of recovering the area around Cambrai from the French and restoring it to the Empire. Edward's allies failed to arrive on time, and it was not until September that his army gathered. After a desultory attempt to take Cambrai, the army moved into France and spread destruction in the hope of provoking Philip to come to battle. By mid-October the allied lords were becoming restless and they were on the point of dispersing to return home when the prospect of battle persuaded them to stay. The French and English armies gathered near the town of La Capelle, with Edward in a strong defensive position. In the event, the French melted away and Edward's allies departed for home.

So far Flanders had remained neutral as the count had maintained a difficult balance between loyalty to the King of France and widespread internal opposition to his policy. However, Jacob van Artevelde, a powerful merchant from Ghent, had lent money to Edward and in return had secured the removal of restrictions on the import of English wool which was so important to Flanders. By late 1339 Artevelde had become *de facto* ruler of Flanders and the count had fled to France. A problem for Edward and Artevelde was that if the Flemings fought for Edward they would be in breach of their allegiance to their overlord the King of France. The way around this problem was for Flanders to recognize Edward as King of France, and in Ghent in January 1340 Edward formally proclaimed his claim to the French crown.

English Successes in Flanders and Brittany – The Treaty of Malestroit
Edward returned to England to raise further subsidies, having expended huge sums during 1339 to pay and encourage his allies. In late June 1340 he set sail once again for Flanders. This was, on the face of it, a risky expedition. The French had had the upper hand at sea so far in the war, and a large fleet, including galleys furnished and crewed by the Genoese, had been assembled at Sluys in anticipation of Edward's return. Naval battles of the period were little different from combat ashore, with men boarding enemy ships to engage in hand-to-hand fighting. As on land, archers provided the English with a powerful weapon. The French chose to remain in harbour with ships chained together to await the English. In doing so they sacrificed their ability to manoeuvre while Edward's ships were free to do so and optimize the use of their archers. The result was a crushing English victory in the first large-scale encounter of the war.

The success at Sluys brought in its train a treaty for Edward with Flanders, Hainault and Brabant. The main objective for the coming campaign was to be Tournai. The town was duly besieged while King Philip watched events from a distance. He failed to come to the relief of the town and after six weeks it seemed close to surrender. However,

Edward was faced with problems holding his allies together and he had little option but to agree to a one year truce, the Truce of Esplechin, to run from September 1340. Early the next year Edward's appointment as the emperor's vicar was withdrawn. The alliance collapsed, bringing to a close two years of war with little to show for the huge sums dispensed by the English exchequer.

In April 1341 the death of John III, Duke of Brittany, led to a disputed succession for the dukedom between John de Montfort and Charles de Blois. Initially, the struggle was a side-show but in early 1342 Edward III acceded to a request for help from Joan of Flanders on behalf of her husband John de Montfort, who was languishing in prison in Paris. An English force duly arrived in Brittany in May 1341, relieving the siege of Hennebout where Joan was holed up. A further English force, under the command of the Earl of Northampton who had been appointed Edward's lieutenant in Brittany, arrived in Brest in July. Northampton advanced to Morlaix and after an unsuccessful assault settled down to besiege the town. Charles de Blois came to its relief in late September, and in the first major land engagement of the war the Earl of Northampton drove off the relieving force. More English troops were to follow, with Edward arriving at Brest in person at the end of October 1342. The threat to the French was now such that it drew in both King Philip and his eldest son the Duke of Normandy, the future King John II. It looked in January 1343 as though there would be a set-piece battle between the French and the English, but once again this was not to be. Later that month the intervention of ambassadors of Pope Clement VI secured the Truce of Malestroit. The truce, which permitted the English and de Montfort's supporters to keep their gains, was intended to last for three years until September 1346.

A Return to War

In the next two years there were frequent outbreaks of fighting, and finally in June 1345 Edward renounced the truce. With the resumption of war Edward conceived a three-pronged attack on France: Northampton from Brittany, the Earl of Derby in the south-west and the king from Flanders. Edward crossed to Flanders, but here his plans came to nothing following the assassination of Artevelde during a riot in Ghent in July 1345. However, that month the Earl of Northampton, accompanied by John de Montfort who had escaped from France the month before, returned to Brittany. The fighting continued through the winter and into 1346 with the English taking a number of towns, and in June 1346 Sir John Dagworth won a remarkable victory against superior numbers at St-Pol-de-Léon. Derby landed in Bayonne more or less simultaneously with Northumberland arriving in Brittany in June 1345 and embarked on an aggressive campaign from the outset, capturing a number of key towns including Bergerac on the Dordogne, and La Réole and Aiguillon on the Garonne. In October 1345 he also defeated a substantially larger French army at Auberoche. The success of Derby drew the Duke of Normandy south, who elected to attempt to retake Aiguillon and settled down to besiege the town in April 1346. The landing of Edward III in Normandy in July left Philip in a difficult position. John, Duke of Normandy, was in the south-west with a substantial force facing a relatively minor threat while the major challenge to the French developed in the north. The Duke of Normandy was recalled, but he was anxious to complete the siege before he departed. In the event he left for the north without taking the town, but he did not leave until 20 August, too late to be able to join his father's army at the Battle of Crécy.

The Crécy Campaign
While Northumberland and Derby continued with their operations during 1346, Edward revised his plans. Two further armies were now envisaged, one to be led by Edward III and a further army drawn from his Flemish allies and led by Sir Hugh Hastings. The destination of Edward's army was announced as Gascony, with the assumed aim being to assist in raising the siege of Aiguillon. However, this was disinformation intended to confuse the French, and once the army was at sea the true destination was revealed as Normandy. Godefroy d'Harcourt, a disaffected Norman noble in Edward's service, may have proposed the landing in his ancestral lands of the Cotentin peninsula, but another factor may have been the historical link between England and the duchy through its possession by English kings in the twelfth century. Whatever the reason, Edward's fleet made land-fall off St-Vaast on 12 July 1346. The subsequent march through France and the Battle of Crécy, fought a little over six weeks later on 26 August 1346, are described later in this guide.

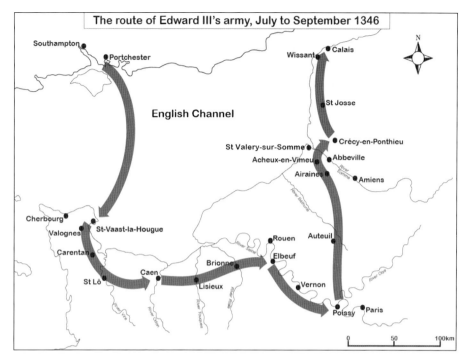

The Crécy Campaign.

From Crécy to Brétigny

In the aftermath of Crécy Derby kept the pressure on the French and in September and October 1346 struck north as far as Poitiers, but the main theatre of operations remained the north. From Crécy-en-Ponthieu Edward III moved north with the objective of laying siege to Calais. On 4 September the first English troops approached the town. Over the next months considerable resources and determination were required to bring the siege to a successful conclusion. Late in July 1347 Philip approached with a large army to relieve the town, and issued a challenge to Edward. The English accepted the challenge but as so often in earlier years the French army faded away. The last hope for the garrison and the inhabitants had gone and the town surrendered. It was to remain an English town for more than 200 years until its surrender to the French in 1558 in the reign of Queen Mary.

In September 1347 a truce was agreed, initially until June of the following year. Although there was sporadic fighting in Brittany, the Calais Pale and Gascony during the formal respite in hostilities, the truce was extended several times until it finally collapsed in 1355. The focus now turned to Gascony, where the French king's lieutenant, the Count of Armagnac, was making worrying incursions into English Aquitaine. Edward III despatched the Black Prince to Bordeaux, and between October and December 1355 he swept across the Languedoc as far as the Mediterranean before returning to Bordeaux. The following year he moved north and at the Battle of Poitiers in September 1356 won another great victory over the French. Poitiers was arguably the closest that the English came to winning a decisive battle during the Hundred Years War, with the French king, since 1350 John II, captured and France thrown into chaos. John was taken to England in May 1357 and negotiations began to secure a lasting peace. It required a further English invasion, led once again by Edward III, in 1359 and 1360 to finally compel the French to agree terms, enshrined in the Treaty of Brétigny which was ratified in Calais in October 1360.

The Peace of Brétigny
Under the Treaty of Brétigny, in addition to Edward and John trading sovereignty over Aquitaine for the English claim to the French crown, huge tracts of south-western France were ceded to Edward. Thus, the first phase of war left the English under Edward III in the ascendancy, but, due to the failure to implement all of its provisions, the Treaty of Brétigny, instead of providing the opportunity for a lasting peace, sowed the seeds for a renewal of war. On John's death in 1364 a substantial proportion of his ransom, agreed as part of the treaty, remained unpaid. The outstanding sum was to remain an issue between England and France, and its settlement was an objective in Henry V's negotiations with the French fifty years later.

The French Recovery, 1369–1389
Charles V succeeded John II in 1364. He had been a party to the Treaty of Brétigny, but since the joint renunciations, of sovereignty over Aquitaine by John and by Edward of his claim to the French crown, had not been ratified he refused to be bound by them. From Charles' accession there was a steady deterioration in relations between France and England, and in 1367, at Nájera in Spain, an Anglo-Gascon army led by the Black Prince in support of Pedro the Cruel's claim to the throne of Castile defeated the other claimant, Henry of Trastámara and his Franco-Castilian army. Pedro reneged on his commitment to fund this campaign, and the Black Prince, who since 1363 had been Prince

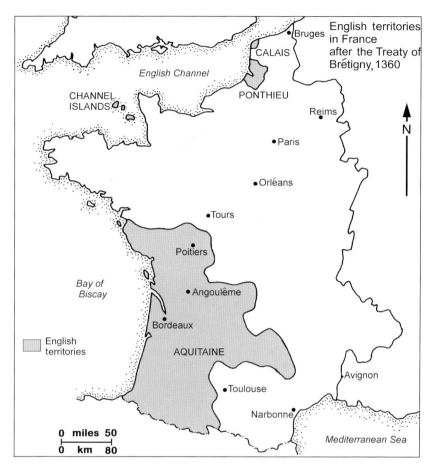

of Aquitaine, had to resort to increased taxation on his subjects in Aquitaine. This resulted in considerable discontent, and in 1368 the Count of Armagnac, whose lands were within the newly expanded Aquitaine, appealed a dispute with the Black Prince to King Charles. Aware that hearing the appeal amounted to a rejection of English claims to sovereignty over Aquitaine, Charles nevertheless issued a summons for the prince to appear in Paris in 1369. The prince failed to attend and the war was renewed.

Charles V was too astute to repeat the experiences of his grandfather and father at the battles of Crécy and Poitiers, and he avoided set-piece battles. His strategy was to harass English armies and gradually push back the boundaries of English-held territory by retaking towns and castles. He was aided by a shrewd and effective commander, Bertrand du Guesclin, Constable of France, and by the time of Charles V's death in 1380 the English possessions had been reduced to the Calais Pale and a coastal strip near Bordeaux.

An Uneasy Truce, 1389–1415

The war continued, without either side making significant advances, until the Truce of Leulinghem in 1389. Negotiations to find a permanent peace dragged on but without success, and in 1396, to forestall the risk of a return to war, an extension to the truce was agreed. The truce was cemented by the marriage of Richard II to Charles VI's daughter Isabella. However, trouble was in the wind, and in 1399 Henry Bolingbroke, son of John of Gaunt, usurped his cousin Richard II to become Henry IV. The French would not recognize Henry as the lawful King of England, but they did agree that the truce of 1396 would remain in force. Henry had his hands full at home with rebellions and trouble in Scotland and Wales, and the French, while stopping short of formally re-opening hostilities, missed no opportunity to create difficulties for the English including incursions into Aquitaine, support for the Scots, recognition of Owen Glendower as Prince of Wales, and tacit support for acts of piracy against English shipping. From 1404 until early 1407 there were more determined, but unsuccessful, attempts to drive the English out of Aquitaine. Within the French camp, Charles VI suffered from sporadic bouts of mental illness which, although never making him totally incapable of ruling, left a major weakness at the heart of French government. This weakness was exacerbated by jockeying for power and feuding between the Duke of Orléans and his supporters, later known as the Armagnacs, and the Burgundians led by Duke John the Fearless. The Duke of Orléans, an erstwhile friend of Henry Bolingbroke while he had been in exile in France during the latter years of the reign of Richard II, turned violently against Henry after his usurpation of Richard, and he was the leading protagonist in attempts to drive the English from Aquitaine. The assassination of the Duke of Orléans in 1407 at the instigation of John the Fearless, successor to Philip the Bold as Duke of Burgundy, relieved the pressure on the English in Aquitaine but also resulted in a period of political instability and complex diplomatic relationships for the rest of the reign of Henry IV.

A triangular relationship emerged between the Armagnacs, the Burgundians and the English. Both French factions tried to gain English support as they manoeuvred for internal power, and the English attempted to exploit the weaknesses within France for their own ends. France descended into civil war during 1411 and 1412, with the English first of all intervening with an army led by the Earl of Arundel supporting the Duke of Burgundy and Charles VI against the rebel Armagnacs. In 1412 Henry IV, in response to a tempting offer from the Armagnacs which included recognition of English sovereignty over Aquitaine, sent an English army of 4,000 men led by the Duke of Clarence to support the rebels. However, by the time Clarence landed, the rebels, Charles VI and the Duke of Burgundy had come to terms and the competing factions were again at peace.

In March 1413 Henry V succeeded to the throne on the death of Henry IV. Because of his father's usurpation of Richard II and the history of rebellions during the reign of Henry IV, the new king could not feel entirely secure on his throne. However, the situation in France was even more precarious. In early 1414 the Duke of Burgundy had fallen from grace and been declared a traitor, and France once more descended into civil war with Charles VI, the dauphin and the Armagnacs launching a war against the Duke of Burgundy. Meanwhile, Henry had agreed a ten-year truce with the Duke of Brittany, declaring the duke to be an ally. Henry V had inherited from his father a campaign in Aquitaine being waged against the Armagnacs. This fighting came to a halt in early 1414, with a truce agreed to last for twelve months and applicable throughout France. Simultaneously Henry was putting out feelers for a lasting peace, with terms which included his marriage to Catherine de Valois, the daughter of Charles VI. With France in disarray due to internecine fighting, Henry felt emboldened enough by May 1414 to start to press his territorial claims on the French king. At about the same time, in parallel with his negotiations with Charles VI, he also started negotiating an alliance with the Duke of Burgundy to include mutual aid through the provision of men-at-arms and archers and a marriage to the duke's daughter. The Duke of Burgundy was prepared to help Henry conquer lands held by the Armagnac lords, but he would not go so far as to enter into an alliance against Charles VI or the dauphin.

The mark of Edward III's prosecution of the war can be seen in

Henry's demand for the restitution by Charles VI of lands granted under the Treaty of Brétigny, and the payment of the 1.6 million *écus* outstanding from the treaty for John II's ransom. He now went further, however, demanding lordship over Normandy, Touraine, Maine and Anjou, and the homage of Brittany and Flanders and marriage to Charles' daughter Catherine with a dowry of two million *écus*. Henry's hope was that with the danger of an Anglo-Burgundian alliance hanging over them, Charles VI and his advisers could be pressurized into accepting these terms. The French were certainly concerned over the English negotiations with the Duke of Burgundy, but they were not prepared to go as far as Henry wanted. His ambassadors returned empty-handed to England in October.

A Return to War, 1415–1444

Meanwhile, Henry had begun to prepare for war. Parliament had agreed to grant taxes to support his policy, but it wanted Henry to continue to negotiate. In pursuit of a negotiated peace, the truce, due to expire in January 1415, had been extended until May, and English ambassadors crossed to France once more in February. By the time of the arrival of the English negotiating team, Charles VI and the Duke of Burgundy had come to terms and agreed the Treaty of Arras. The treaty banned any alliances with the English which could be prejudicial to the interests of the French crown. When the negotiations reopened in March, Henry's ambassadors presented much-reduced territorial demands and progress was being made on the marriage between Henry and Catherine. The French, although their position had been much strengthened by the Duke of Burgundy's accommodation with the king, were ready to move some way towards Henry's demand over territories in Aquitaine. However, they linked this concession to withdrawal of the English claim for the sum outstanding from John II's ransom. The English ambassadors withdrew from negotiations towards the end of March, declaring that they did not have the authority to agree the terms on offer. Henry had so far failed to exploit French divisions, but he continued to try to come to an accord with the Duke of Burgundy during the spring and summer and the French continued to harbour fears of an Anglo-Burgundian alliance. They also sought to delay Henry's preparation for war, and French ambassadors crossed to England in June. Negotiations, which were held with Henry in person, broke down acrimoniously and the ambassadors returned to France in early July.

As negotiations and preparations for war continued, Henry was acutely aware that his hold on the throne was insecure. There had been remarks by the French ambassadors that not only did he have no right to the French crown but also that they should be negotiating with descendants of Richard II and not Henry, and there was an apparent plot against him on the eve of his departure from the Solent on 1 August 1415 (the Southampton Plot), which resulted in the summary execution of the Earl of Cambridge, Henry Lord Scrope and Sir Thomas Grey.

Henry had intended to assemble his army by 1 July, but delays in mustering troops and gathering enough shipping delayed departure until 11 August. The landing was to be made in Normandy, probably with the objective of taking the duchy to strengthen Henry's bargaining position. Harfleur was the initial target, a useful bridgehead in northern France which would also deny the French use of an important fortified naval base which had been used to launch attacks against the coast of England and on English shipping. Having taken Harfleur, Henry marched north-east towards Calais and safety. On reaching the Somme he found the ford at Blanchetaque too well defended by the French and he marched up-river until he was able to cross. He turned once again towards Calais and confronted and defeated the French at Agincourt. After his victory he continued to Calais and returned to England.

The Battle of Agincourt is popularly seen as the greatest English victory in the Middle Ages. However, despite the magnitude of the victory it was not decisive. Edward III, Henry's great-grandfather, had been able to follow up his victory at Crécy with the siege and capture of Calais, and Edward's son the Black Prince had captured John II at Poitiers, thus giving his father perhaps the closest that the English were to come to a decisive victory during the Hundred Years War. After Agincourt Charles VI remained at large, and Henry V did not have the means to follow up his victory that year. However, it did secure Henry's position on the throne and he could pursue his obsession with France unchallenged at home. He could now return to England and capitalize on his success and plan for the future.

During 1416 the Holy Roman Emperor Sigismund, who had

initially offered to mediate between the French and the English, recognized Henry's claim to the French throne. Later in the year Sigismund and Henry met the Duke of Burgundy at Calais. Henry was encouraged that, while the Duke of Burgundy would not go so far as to recognize him as King of France, he would not stand in his way, and in August 1417 Henry set off again for France. His aim was to conquer the Duchy of Normandy and use it to enforce his claims. By the end of September Caen was in English hands. Other towns, including Bayeux, fell soon after and the conquest continued with Rouen, the greatest Norman city, falling in January 1419. The Duke of Burgundy was meanwhile taking advantage of the English operations to launch attacks against the Armagnacs. However, there was ambiguity in the Burgundian position and there were occasions when English and Burgundian troops clashed. The French were well aware that their disunity was playing into the hands of Henry V, and attempts were made to resolve the differences between the factions. In September the Duke of Burgundy met the dauphin. Heated discussions ensued and Duke John the Fearless was murdered by a member of the dauphin's party, thus precipitating the very event that the dauphin wished to avoid: pushing Burgundy, now ruled by the new duke, Philip the Good, into the arms of the English. In December 1419 Henry and Philip agreed to wage war together against the dauphin. They also agreed that if Henry succeeded in his pursuit of his claim to the French crown, the Duke of Burgundy would be his lieutenant for his French domains.

Henry now turned his attention to King Charles VI with negotiations which concluded with the Treaty of Troyes in May 1420. Under the treaty the dauphin was declared a bastard and his claim to the succession set aside. Henry was to be heir to Charles VI and to be regent of France during the remainder of Charles' life. He was to retain the Duchy of Normandy by right of conquest in the meantime, and his entitlement to hold Aquitaine without homage was recognized. Little more than a week after the treaty Henry married Charles' daughter Catherine.

The dauphin, who was by no means powerless, had been consolidating his position. In response to the dauphin invoking the 'auld alliance' with Scotland a number of Scots had entered his service, and at Easter 1421 the Duke of Clarence was killed when he was defeated at Baugé by a Franco-Scottish army. In June Henry V returned to France. In December Henry's heir, the future Henry VI, was born, but before a year had passed Henry V died of dysentery in August 1422. Less than two months later Charles VI followed him to the grave. The infant Henry VI was proclaimed King of England and France.

Henry V's untimely death at the age of thirty-five left his brother the Duke of Bedford as regent in France. Under his regency there were further English victories, but the duke was faced with a range of problems as he struggled to build on Henry's legacy and consolidate English rule in France. He and the Duke of Burgundy controlled large areas of France, but outside these areas France was loyal to the dauphin, and Bedford struggled to make further inroads into this territory. He also faced growing discontent from Henry VI's subjects in France compelled to pay taxes to support the war and a similar reluctance at home to pay for the continuing fighting. Difficulties with his allies compounded his problems. The Duke of Brittany moved back and forth between the French and English causes and the Duke of Burgundy was reluctant to pursue the war vigorously.

Then in 1429 Joan of Arc came onto the scene, bringing a change of fortune for the French. The siege of Orléans was broken in May, and the retreating English army was defeated at the Battle of Patay the following month. The dauphin, at Joan's urging, went to Rheims and was crowned and anointed as Charles VII, giving a further boost to his standing and French morale. The capture of Joan in 1430 and her subsequent trial and execution in 1431 offered the prospect of restored English fortunes, and the Duke of Bedford brought Henry VI to Paris to be crowned King of France in December. However, lack of funds from England to prosecute the war, and the continuing necessity of imposing taxes on the inhabitants of Normandy, led to increasing discontent among the population and an erosion of English control. The following year the Duke of Burgundy was beginning to look for ways to break with the English. In 1435 the Duke of Bedford died, and only two weeks after his death Philip the Good finally made peace with Charles VII.

The Truce of Tours, 1444–1449, and the Defeat of the English
The war continued with the French making inroads into English-held lands and by 1444 the areas held by the English had been reduced to

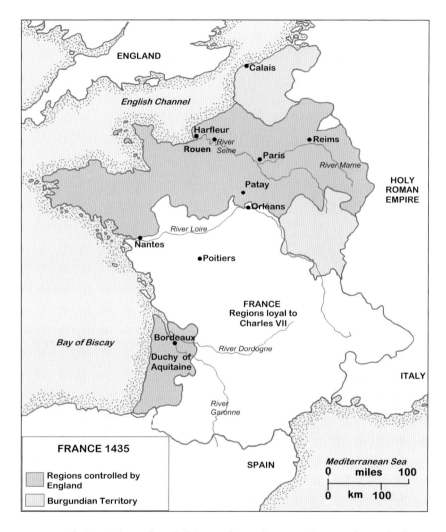

ENGLAND

Calais

English Channel

Harfleur
River
Rouen Seine
Reims
Paris
River Marne

HOLY
ROMAN
EMPIRE

Patay

Orléans

River Loire

Nantes

Poitiers

FRANCE
Regions loyal to
Charles VII

Bay of Biscay

Bordeaux
River Dordogne

Duchy of
Aquitaine

ITALY

River
Garonne

FRANCE 1435

SPAIN

Mediterranean Sea

Regions controlled by
England

Burgundian Territory

0   miles   100

0   km   100

part of Aquitaine, the Calais enclave, Lower Normandy and the County of Maine. But by now both sides were ready for peace, and the Truce of Tours was agreed. The truce collapsed in 1449, and the English were rapidly swept aside. By April 1450 all of Henry V's gains in northern France had gone. The French now turned their attention to Bordeaux and Aquitaine, and in July 1453 an Anglo-Gascon army was routed at Castillon, the last battle of the Hundred Years War. Three months later Bordeaux surrendered and the war was over.

At first sight it may seem strange that the English kings should win the three great battles of Crécy, Poitiers and Agincourt, as well as many less well known battles, and yet lose the war. However, with the benefit of hindsight it is difficult to see how English kings could have held on to power in France. France was significantly richer and more populous than England. Edward III overcame these imbalances in population and wealth through victories on the battlefield at Crécy and Poitiers, the exploitation of internal divisions in France, and his effective use of contracted armies. Of all the English kings during the war it was Edward III, with the successive victories of Crécy and Poitiers, and the Treaty of Brétigny, who came closest to bringing the war to a successful conclusion, but even if the treaty had held in the longer run the overall imbalance between the two countries would surely in due course have brought a renewal of war and the defeat of England. As it was, the inherent weakness of the English position became apparent after the collapse of the Treaty of Brétigny in 1369, when Edward now had to hold vastly expanded territories while Charles V avoided pitched battles and recovered towns and castles slowly but surely. By Henry V's time the French internal divisions were even more acute than during Edward III's reign, and in alliance with the Duke of Burgundy he was able to take advantage of French weakness to conquer and hold wide swathes of territory. However, in Henry VI's reign holding these lands imposed an intolerable burden of taxation both at home and in the English territories in France. In addition, French military reforms came to fruition under Charles VII, resulting in a more professional army which made good use of its artillery to reduce the last English strongholds and bring Charles' army victory at Castillon. The internal divisions within France were also gradually mastered. Once this process had been completed and French resources could be effectively used, the expulsion of the English from France was probably inevitable. Within two years of the Battle of Castillon England became embroiled in the Wars of the Roses, and with the energies of English kings and the nobility turned inwards, there was no way back to achieve the goals set by Edward III more than a century earlier.

Tour One

St-Vaast-la-Hougue
to Caen

This tour starts at St-Vaast-la-Hougue, where Edward III and his army disembarked on 12 July 1346, and continues to Caen, plundered by the English army before they broke camp and moved on from the town on 31 July. It covers a distance of about 160km.

What Happened

Edward III had arrived at Portchester on 1 June 1346 and waited while his fleet gathered. By the end of the month around 1,000 ships had

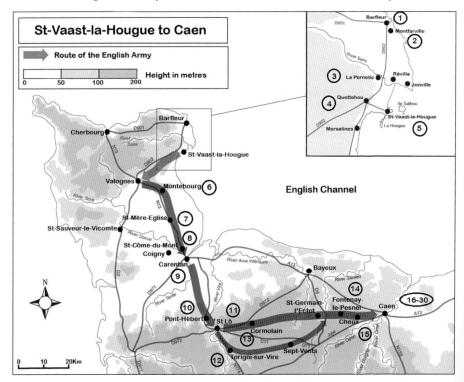

been assembled, enough to carry the army of around 14,000 men, comprising 2,800 knights and men-at-arms, 3,000 mounted archers, and 8,000 infantry, of whom 5,000 were archers. To provide mounts for the knights, men-at-arms and mounted archers, there would have been at least 10,000 horses to be transported. Medieval armies, however, included not just fighting men but also a wide range of camp followers and men of many civilian trades. With this army were miners, masons, carpenters, tent-makers, blacksmiths, farriers, surgeons, clerks and servants. The ships were provisioned for two weeks, sufficient for the passage to Bordeaux in Gascony. The expectation seems to have been that the destination was indeed Gascony, but this was a cover story to attempt to confound the French. The real destination was shrouded in great secrecy because a landing in Bordeaux would have been without risk of opposition, whereas a landing in French territory would be very risky if the destination were known and opposition could be assembled. Around 20 June Sir Hugh Hastings was appointed as the king's lieutenant in Flanders and a small force marshalled to go with him. No secret was made of his destination, and his mission was to work with the Flemings who had declared that they would assist King Edward. As King Philip VI started to get wind of what was in store he turned to the Scots to try to persuade them to take action in the north.

The fleet sailed on 28 June, still under a cloak of secrecy as to the destination, and with the ships masters carrying sealed orders concerning the destination. These orders were to be opened in the case of the fleet being dispersed by adverse weather. Unfavourable winds disrupted the start of the expedition and the ships reassembled south of Portsmouth to await more favourable conditions. It was only on 11 July that the fleet finally set off for Normandy, anchoring off the beach south of St-Vaast-la-Hougue (Point 5) before dawn the next day. The bay south of St-Vaast is well sheltered, with shallow beaches which would have made the landings relatively trouble-free, although timing would have been important since high spring tides in particular cover the beach completely with the sea lapping against the rocky foreshore. First ashore were the Earl of Warwick and Godefroy d'Harcourt, who had been banished from France two years earlier and who held lands around St-Sauveur-le-Vicomte and towards Carentan on the Cotentin peninsula. They landed with 400 men-at-arms and 1,100 archers to establish and protect the beachhead for the subsequent disembarkation of the mass of men, horses, equipment and supplies.

There was no serious opposition to the disembarkation of the English army. The bulk of the French forces in Normandy were some distance away north of the Seine. The French king's senior representative, the marshal Robert Bertrand, had summoned local men of military age to muster in their home districts. The muster in St-Vaast-la-Hougue had to be abandoned because of the English landing. In addition, a company of Genoese crossbowmen, who had been based at St-Vaast-la-Hougue since April, had deserted a few days before the landings because they were unpaid. Ships, including eight intended for the defence of St-Vaast-la-Hougue, were found abandoned on the beach and burnt by the English. Not only had ships been abandoned but also villagers fled and took refuge as the English approached, adding to the marshal's problems in finding men. With all these difficulties his resources were very limited, and the best he could do was make a desultory attack with a few hundred men who were driven off by those from the English fleet who were already ashore.

The king landed at around mid-day on 12 July and, it is said, tripped and fell, hitting his head which provoked a nose-bleed. Some saw this as an ill-omen, but the king retorted that on the contrary it showed that the land was ready to receive him. Having climbed a hill nearby, the king knighted a number of young noblemen, including the sixteen-year-old Prince of Wales, the Black Prince, and the Earl of Salisbury. In addition, Godefroy d'Harcourt paid homage to Edward for his lands in Normandy. It has been suggested that these ceremonies were held in the church of St Vigor in the village of Quettehou (Point 4), which stands on the ridge 3km west of St-Vaast-la-Hougue. It has also been suggested that the king then moved north 3km to La Pernelle (Point 3), standing on one of the highest points on the escarpment with clear views north towards Barfleur (Point 1) and south to the landing beaches, to survey the surrounding countryside and the coastline.

On his first day ashore the king ordered that the people of Normandy and their property were to be respected. In particular, towns and manors were not to be burnt, churches and holy places were not to be sacked and the lives of the old, women and children were to be spared since they were his French subjects. Transgressors risked life and limb, and a reward of forty shillings was offered to bring before the king any offender caught red-handed. In theory the constable and the marshals should have enforced the king's order, but in reality the army plundered and burned far and wide from the start and even as the king was looking out from La Pernelle he may well have seen the villages of Réville and Jonville, just to the north of St-Vaast, burning. On the following day, 13 July, St-Vaast-la-Hougue was burnt and the king moved to the nearby village of Morsalines, now a small settlement with a population of around 200, where he lodged in an inn. On 14 July elements of the army, together with some ships from the English fleet, reached the port of Barfleur, 10km north of St-Vaast-la-Hougue, and the town, further abandoned ships and the surrounding countryside were burnt and pillaged. Prisoners were also taken.

There was some sporadic and un-coordinated resistance, with the Earl of Warwick and his company, who were attacked while taking over an inn, amongst those who met resistance. However, the earl is reported to have fought honourably and driven off the enemy despite being outnumbered. Other inhabitants did not resist and withdrew to walled towns, joined a flood of refugees heading south or stayed put, accepting the arrival of the English as something they could not oppose.

There is a stretch of land immediately beyond the beaches about 800m deep and extending for 3km on both sides of Morsalines before the terrain starts to climb. This would have provided an ideal area to unload and organize stores, equipment, men and horses, and five days were spent here preparing for the coming campaign. These preparations included the baking of bread. In view of the scale of the operation five days was by no means a long period for completing the disembarkation and organization for the onward march. In addition, horses need time to adjust after a sea voyage and it would have been prudent not to have tried to move off too quickly. The Black Prince was to find to his cost in 1355 that pushing horses too hard after a sea passage could result in many deaths. The king's plan was to march east, parallel to the coast, and then to move up the valley of the Seine to invade the Île de France. In doing so he probably intended to relieve the pressure on the small English armies already in France, but with an expedition of this size he must have had a grander objective in mind.

It seems very likely from the outset that he wanted to draw Philip into battle. Furthermore, judging by the subsequent conduct of the campaign, his plan to join with Hugh Hastings and the arrangements he made for reinforcements to be sent to Le Crotoy, he may have had the County of Ponthieu in mind as the place for battle from the outset.

The army was divided in a conventional manner into three divisions for the march. The vanguard was under the nominal command of the sixteen-year-old Black Prince but in reality was led by the Earls of Northampton, the constable, and Warwick, the marshal, who were his senior advisers. The king commanded the centre and Thomas Hatfield, the Bishop of Durham, led the rear-guard with the Earls of Suffolk, Arundel and Huntingdon. Two hundred ships, the remainder being discharged from royal service, were to follow the army along the coast. Before setting out east, however, the fleet moved around the Cotentin peninsula, with landing parties destroying villages as they went. Of the castles in the area, only the garrison of Cherbourg stayed at its post and held out. In Cherbourg the twelfth-century Augustinian abbey of Notre Dame du Voeu, founded by Henry I's daughter Matilda, suffered one of many assaults in its life and was burned by the marauding troops.

Edward's army finally broke camp on 18 July and started out on its march, climbing away from the coastal plain and up onto the higher ground, passing through thickly wooded countryside, some of which remains in the Bois du Rabey astride the D902 to the west of Quettehou. The first destination was the undefended town of Valognes, 15km from Morsalines. The inhabitants came out to meet the king, pleading for him to spare their lives and property. The king stayed in a house of the Dukes of Normandy and the Black Prince in the house of the Bishop of Coutances. The king restated his orders for his men to respect the property of his Norman subjects, but again to no avail. The men took what plunder they wished and left the town in flames when they moved on next morning.

From Valognes the English moved on to St-Côme-du-Mont (Point 8), which stands near the river Douve, on 19 July. Around 15km south-west of Valognes lies St-Sauveur-le-Vicomte, the ancestral home of Godefroy d'Harcourt, and, with the ostensible aim of protecting the right flank, Godefroy d'Harcourt set off in this direction only to find that the castle was in ruins, having been destroyed by his arch-enemy

The river Douve just to the south of St-Côme-du-Mont. (Peter Hoskins)

the French marshal Robert Bertrand three years before. The remainder of the army set off more directly towards St-Côme-du-Mont and is reported to have passed Montebourg (Point 6) with its fine Benedictine abbey on its left, although there are accounts of the town being burnt and looted. On the road to St-Côme-du-Mont is Ste-Mère-Eglise (Point 7) which, apart from its church, was totally destroyed during the Hundred Years War, and subsequently rebuilt on adjacent ground. The march to St-Côme-du-Mont would have been easy going across the most gentle of undulating terrain with no rivers of any consequence to slow progress. There had been a bridge over the Douve just beyond St-Côme-du-Mont since at least the twelfth century which could have been of great help to the English if it had been intact. However, the bridge had been broken and had to be rebuilt overnight before the army crossed the river the following day and advanced on Carentan (Point 9). According to local tradition the bridge had been destroyed by local inhabitants and St-Côme-du-Mont was burnt down in reprisal, but it is more likely that the destruction was no more than part of the prevailing pattern of looting and burning.

In the fourteenth century there was marshland on the approach to the river and extending well beyond the Douve and Carentan. Despite drainage in more modern times the area of marshland is readily identifiable. The army had to advance on narrow paths across this marshland with water on both sides towards the town which stands on a narrow spur of ground 25m above the surrounding marsh. The town was defended by walls with wide ditches on three sides and the river to the north behind the church, and the garrison included Genoese mercenaries willing to fight. Thus, this would have been an ideal place to disrupt the English advance, but the bourgeois decided to surrender and there was no opposition within the town. Furthermore, after a brief struggle, the castle at Carentan, in which King John of England had stayed frequently, was surrendered to the English. Two Norman knights, Raoul de Verdun and Nicholas de Groussy, who were protégés of Godefroy d'Harcourt, were left in command of a mixed Anglo-Norman garrison. The town was pillaged and burnt, with over 1,000 inhabitants said to have been killed, and the houses of notables and the defences deliberately destroyed. One account relates that this destruction and pillaging was a result of the fury of Edward III at the death of three French lords in his service, Tesson, Bacon and Percy. However, again this may have been simply part of the pattern of general destruction. Whatever the truth of the matter, Edward was concerned about the consequences of poor discipline and ordered that food should not be wasted. The castle was subsequently retaken by supporters of Philip VI, and de Verdun and de Groussy were captured and taken to Paris where they were decapitated for treason in December 1346.

From Carentan Edward's army now followed the causeway through the marsh towards St-Lô. The land here climbs almost imperceptibly from sea-level near Carentan to 70m before descending more steeply to the valley of the Vire, where the bridge at Pont-Hébert (Point 10) had been destroyed by Robert Bertrand, who hoped to make a stand at St-Lô (Point 11), 6km beyond the river. He put his men in the town and enthusiastic townspeople manned the walls and set about repairing defences which had been neglected. However, no attempt was made to impede the crossing of the river when the Black Prince reached Pont-Hébert on 21 July and the English set about repairing the bridge unopposed. While the army waited for the repairs, Edward III is

Marshland in the vicinity of Carentan, with the church of Notre Dame in the background. The marsh is considerably drier than it would have been in the Middle Ages due to modern drainage and the construction of canals. (Peter Hoskins)

said to have stayed at the château of Esglandes 2km west of Pont-Hébert; the castle has long since gone and only a bell-tower and cemetery from the parish church remain to mark the spot. Once the bridge had been repaired the English crossed the river the next day. St-Lô stands on high ground to the east of a sweeping ox-bow bend in the Vire, and the English army, approaching from the north, would have faced impressive-looking ramparts. Perhaps the poor state of these ramparts gave Bertrand little confidence in their efficacy, and he decided that discretion was the better part of valour and withdrew, leaving the English to take the town.

Over the gates of St-Lô the arriving English found the skulls of three Norman knights executed for treason by Philip VI for having fought for Edward III in Brittany three years before. It is said that the skulls were taken down and given a proper burial, possibly as a private act by Harcourt. The same pattern as hitherto was repeated, with the rich market town being subject to looting and destruction, with one

Most of the existing ramparts of St-Lô date from after the fourteenth century, but nevertheless they give a good impression of the strength of the town. (Peter Hoskins)

chronicler reporting that at least 1,000 barrels of wine were found in the town. The inhabitants had stayed put in anticipation of the town being defended, and were now unable to escape. Some were shipped back to England for ransom and others were killed.

Once beyond St-Lô the army climbed steadily onto higher ground with more pronounced undulations than hitherto, advancing on a wide front, burning and plundering a swathe of a countryside rich with farms, orchards, cattle and horses, and implementing the classic *chevauchée* tactics of Edward III. Later in the campaign, in a letter to King Philip, Edward summarized the objectives of such operations as being to punish rebels, in other words those who did not recognize his claim to the French throne, to comfort friends and those faithful to him, and to carry on the war as best he could, to his advantage and the loss of his enemies. Underlying these objectives was the overall aim of provoking the French king into giving battle, and the widespread destruction served this purpose by demonstrating that the French king was incapable of fulfilling his duty to protect his people.

Meanwhile the fleet was destroying everything within an 8km strip of coast from Cherbourg to the mouth of the Orne at Ouistreham north of Caen. Over 100 French ships, including 61 prepared for naval service, were burned. The quantity of plunder taken was such that ships were fully loaded and masters started to desert to take their gains home to England. In addition to the desire to take plunder, many in the ships' crews would have been from the English south coast and they would have been only too pleased to exact revenge for recent French attacks on Portsmouth and Southampton.

On 23 July the king gave orders for the army to gather at Torigny-sur-Vire (Point 12), 15km south-east of St-Lô, and Sir Thomas Holland set off with an advance party. However, on the receipt of new intelligence the king changed his plans and moved off to the east to Cormolain (Point 13), where the French constable had lodged the previous night. Some elements of the army probably lodged at Sept-Vents 8km to the south. Those who had gone ahead with Thomas Holland to arrange quartering at Torigny-sur-Vire, including houses for the nobles, withdrew to rejoin the army at Cormolain, burning the town and the intervening countryside as they went.

When the army left Cormolain on 24 July they burnt the town and the surrounding countryside, but some archers were trapped inside a building which they were plundering and suffocated when it was set alight by the French. The army stopped that night near Maupertuis, now the site of a much more modern château and farm, in the village of St-Germain-d'Ectot. The next day the king moved on to Fontenay-le-Pesnel (Point 14), possibly lodging in a monastic cell at Le Cairon 3km south in the village of Vendes. Meanwhile the prince lodged at Cheux (Point 15) 4km further east. Although there are now no traces there is said to have been a fortress here in the fourteenth century.

In its encampments near Fontenay-le-Pesnel the army was 18km west of Caen (Points 16–30). The officials in Caen had heard news of the devastation caused by the English, and the evidence was in front of their eyes as refugees with carts and animals thronged the streets of the town. That evening an English monk, Geoffrey of Maldon, arrived with letters calling on the town to surrender and offering in return to spare the lives of citizens and their goods and homes. The evident inability of Edward III to keep to his terms offered to the citizens of Valognes and St-Côme-du-Mont may well have weighed on the decision of the officials, but in any case the terms were rejected and the Bishop of Bayeux had the unfortunate English friar thrown into prison.

At first light on Wednesday, 26 July the English army started its advance across the flat plain between Fontenay-le-Pesnel and Caen and is said to have established camp on the plains of Ardennes, in the commune of St-Germain-la-Blanche-Herbe 4km west of the town, Couvrechef, now absorbed into the suburb of La Folie-Couvrechef 2km to the north-west, and Hérouville, now in the commune of Hérouville-St-Clair 4km to the north-east. Caen was a large town, second only to Rouen in Normandy, with a population of around 10,000. It had a strong castle to the north, built by William the Conqueror and developed by Henry I of England, but the town was poorly protected with low walls dating from the eleventh century which were poorly maintained. There were eight gates in the walls, and twenty interval towers. A slightly later tower, La Tour Guillaume le Roy, survives on the site of one of these. To the west of the town, whose walls on the eastern side were contiguous with the town ramparts, was the Abbaye aux Hommes and to the east, about 200m beyond the walls but within its own walls, was the Abbaye aux Dames. The ramparts to the south of the town were protected by the river Odon, which flowed approximately where the Boulevard du Maréchal Leclerc runs today.

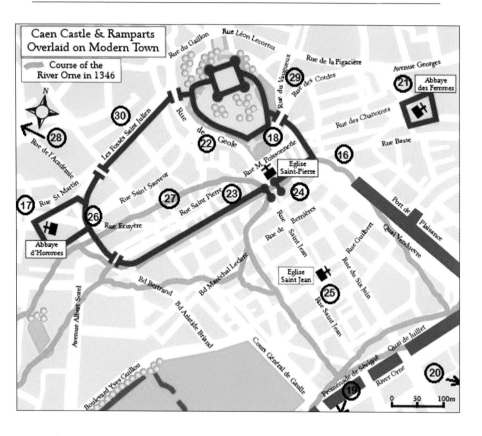

Caen Castle & Ramparts
Overlaid on Modern Town

Course of the
River Orne in 1346

There was a bridge across the Odon, protected by towers on both sides of the river, which led into the rich suburb of the Île St-Jean. This suburb was unwalled but completely surrounded by the river Orne and was orientated along the line of the modern rue St-Jean. There were two gates into the town to the north.

The arrival of the English army came as no surprise and measures had been taken for the defence of Caen. Although the two abbeys were defensible, in particular the Abbaye aux Hommes whose walls had been newly constructed, they were both abandoned for lack of manpower. Inside the town the Count of Eu and the Lord of Tancarville had perhaps 1,500 men, including 300 Genoese crossbowmen under command of the captain of the castle, Robert de Warignies. The garrison of the town had improved the defences as best they could with palisades and trenches to the north and west, and to the south thirty ships and barges had been moored along the banks of the Odon with archers on their decks.

The English advance to Caen was made on a broad front of several kilometres, with the camp followers and non-combatants spread out in front to give the impression of a much larger army than was in fact the case. Their appearance over the brow of the low ridge around the town seems to have caused a change of plan. The Count of Eu and the Lord of Tancarville decided to abandon the old town and place their hopes in the defence of the suburb of the Île- St-Jean to the south, although women of higher rank were taken into the castle for protection along with the Bishop of Bayeux. Other women and children were sent towards Falaise for safety. The decision to concentrate the defence in the Île St-Jean was probably made under pressure from the wealthier residents whose homes and wealth were on the island. Thus, some 200 men-at-arms and 100 Genoese crossbowmen were left to defend the castle and the remainder of the garrison withdrew across the bridge of St Pierre to the Île St-Jean. The defences were weak, with the line of ships on the Odon, the fortified Porte-St-Pierre, and to the south and east only the branches of the river providing protection. Unfortunately the fortifications of the Porte-St-Pierre were orientated to defend the old town to the north and not the Île St-Jean, although a barricade had been erected to the north in an attempt to ameliorate the situation. The problem was exacerbated by the low level of the river because of a dry summer, which allowed men to wade across where ships could normally navigate.

The king advanced towards the south of the town. The Black Prince took a more northerly route, probably across the plain where the airport of Caen-Carpiquet now stands and past the twelfth-century abbey of Ardennes, pillaged in 1417 during the siege of Caen, towards the abandoned Abbaye aux Dames. The assault on Caen began in an uncoordinated fashion when some of the Black Prince's men seized a gate to the old town. The Earl of Warwick entered the town with some men-at-arms and archers. The men converged on the Porte-St-Pierre, burning houses in the vicinity and engaging the defenders in hand-to-hand fighting at the barricade. The king was concerned at this disorderly attack being made before he could concentrate his efforts. He sent the Earl of Northampton and Richard Talbot with some men-at-arms to order Warwick to sound the retreat. Either the signal was ignored by the troops, or Warwick and Northampton decided that it would be better to continue with the combat than to break off the assault. In any case the fighting spread out along the river banks. Two of the boats moored on the river bank were set alight, and others boarded as men forded their way across the river in the face of shooting by the crossbowmen. The defenders at the bridge now found themselves surrounded. Some managed to flee to the old town, and others took temporary refuge in the fortified gate towers. The townspeople joined in the defence as best they could, with the women bringing materials, food and wine to the men. For the French, however, the game was up and, although sporadic fighting continued, men of rank looked for those of appropriate stature to take their surrender. The Count of Eu surrendered to Sir Thomas Holland. The count was subsequently purchased by King Edward. He spent three years in England before returning to France to raise his ransom of 20,000 nobles, but was executed for his pains shortly after his return. In the circumstances it is possible that the ransom was never paid. The surrender of the Lord of Tancarville was accepted by Sir Thomas Daniel, a retainer of the Black Prince. He was held in Wallingford castle until his release in 1348 after payment of his ransom. Several hundred prisoners were taken overall, including some rich citizens. Some 2,500 bodies were said to have been found in the streets after the fighting, with one contemporary estimate putting the number of French casualties at 5,000. In contrast to these figures only one English man-at-arms is known to have been killed, but in view of the nature of the fighting it is likely that casualties among the archers and infantry would have been heavy.

As dusk settled on the town the castle still held, with its 300 men under the command of Robert Bertrand and his brother Guillaume, the Bishop of Bayeux. The following morning, Thursday, 27 July, five men were seen leaving the castle. Three were killed and two were taken prisoner, but little useful information was forthcoming. The message that they were carrying is unknown, but it is likely that the Bertrands would want to get news out that, despite the destruction of the town, the castle remained in safe hands and they would continue to resist. Refugees from Caen may well have fled 30km north-west to Bayeux, spreading the news of the disaster, since later on that Thursday emissaries from the town arrived in Caen offering to surrender Bayeux.

The offer was refused on the grounds that Edward was not yet in a position to protect the town. The representatives were allowed to depart, with the expectation that their offer would be accepted at a later date. On the Friday Edward's men ranged far and wide pillaging and burning. Bayeux seems to have escaped unscathed, but there was clearly alarm in the town, and on Saturday fifteen citizens of Bayeux returned to Caen to finalize the surrender. Before leaving Caen on Monday, 31 July arrangements were made to ship to England the more important prisoners, including sixty knights and 300 rich burgers, and the very considerable booty taken in the town.

The French Response

King Philip VI was in no position to pose a serious challenge to Edward III's invasion. He had summoned men to assemble in June, but the slow process was not going to produce an army of any consequence before August. In addition, the Duke of Normandy was in the south-west trying to take Aiguillon. In the meantime the French forces in the north were limited to scattered garrisons and coastguards, which could not be expected to be any more successful than the marshal's small band of men had been at the time of the landings. The constable, Raoul II, Count of Eu, concentrated his efforts on delaying the progress of the English army once it started to move away from the landing zone, with the objective of stopping it at Caen using the Orne as a natural line of defence. With this in mind the constable transported troops by boat from Harfleur to Caen. The chamberlain, Jean de Melun, Lord of Tancarville, joined the constable and men and stores were sent to the castle in Caen. The marshal sought to delay the English progress while the preparations at Caen were being made. However, his force was not strong enough to have a serious effect on Edward's advance, and Bertrand had to content himself with harassing tactics and the destruction of some bridges on the English route as he withdrew in front of the English. At about the date that the English were reaching Pont-Hébert on 21 July, Hugh Hastings arrived in Flanders. The French now had to divide and while Rouen was designated as the assembly point for the army to counter Edward, a part of their forces was directed to Amiens to hold the Somme against Hastings and the Flemings. Philip VI took the *oriflamme*, a great banner carried in battle when the king was present, and which signified that no quarter would be given and no prisoners taken, at Saint-Denis on 22 July. He then set off slowly down the Seine valley. At about this time he wrote to King David of Scotland to try to persuade the Scots to invade England with the aim of taking the pressure off France. There was some cross-border raiding, but there was no serious attempt at an invasion and at the end of July a two-month truce neutralized the Scottish threat for the time being at least.

The Army on the March

It is difficult to visualize a medieval army on the march, but in the First World War a British army division of 20,000 men with 5,000 or so horses stretched over 25km of road and took seven hours to pass a point. With the poor roads of the fourteenth century Edward's army would have moved on a broad front rather than in a column, and in a dispersed marching order to facilitate foraging from the countryside to supplement rations carried by the troops. Nevertheless this comparison gives some idea of the considerable enterprise of managing a large army on the move.

When Edward set off on his march he had an army of around 14,000 men. On top of this he would have had several thousand non-combatants, including pages and men drawn from many medieval trades. Armourers, fletchers, bowyers, blacksmiths, tent-makers, physicians, clerks, clergy, jugglers and musicians would typically accompany such armies, but we also know that Edward had forty carpenters, his engineers for bridge-building. In addition, there would have been men for handling the cannon, and a large number of carts would have been required to carry supplies. The stock of arrows, perhaps as many as 250,000 carried in barrels, would alone have required a significant number of carts.

Feeding an army of this size was a huge task, and the daily demand would be for 25 tonnes or more of food. An even bigger challenge would be feeding and watering the horses. Knights, esquires, and men-at-arms typically took four, three and two horses on campaign, respectively. Mounted archers would normally have one horse, and some non-combatants would also have horses. There would be others to pull carts and an estimate of 10,000 horses for the army is on the conservative side. The daily needs for food and water for so many horses would have been considerable. Each horse would need about

25kg of fresh grass or 10kg of dry fodder per day. In view of the quantities required it would not be practical to carry dry fodder, so each day some 100 tonnes of dry fodder or several hectares of pasture would have to be found. The water requirements were also demanding, since each horse would drink around 18 litres a day.

Food was brought from England and there would also have been livestock with the army, but it would have been impossible to provision for the entire campaign in this way and Edward's army would have needed to live off the land. With the English army on the move in the late summer, village store-houses could be expected to be replenished from the harvest, and raiding villages would provide some of the needs of the army. However, the French would have tried wherever possible to take supplies into fortified towns, foraging parties would have been harassed, and villagers would have done their best to hide animals and supplies. In addition, destroying crops and killing animals in the path of an advancing army was a common defensive practice. In the early stages of the march, until Lisieux, the French do not seem to have been well enough organized to deny the English their supplies, but as the march progressed the army became increasingly short of food.

The Route by Car

The Barfleur Variant

The main route starts in St-Vaast-la-Hougue, where Edward III's army disembarked. However, a variant, which takes in Barfleur, Montfarville, Réville and La Pernelle, adds only about 10km to the tour. Leave Barfleur (Point 1) on the D902 and after 1.5km turn left onto an unnumbered road to Montfarville (Point 2). Leave the village on an unnumbered road, Rue És Pailles, and join the D155. Follow the D155 and D168 into Réville. From Réville follow the D1 and D328 to the D928. Turn right onto the D928 and then left onto the D328 to La Pernelle (Point 3). Leave La Pernelle on the D328 and then turn left to follow the D125, D26 and D902 to Quettehou (Point 4). Take the D1 to St-Vaast-la-Hougue (Point 5) and rejoin the main route.

The Main Route

Leave St-Vaast-la-Hougue (Point 5) on the D1 towards Quettehou. Just after entering the village turn left and follow the D14 to Morsalines. Turn right onto the D216 and take the first turn to the right after St-Martin-d'Audouville onto the D62. Follow this road to Valognes.

Follow the D974, N13 and again the D974 from Valognes to Montebourg (Point 6). Continue on the D974 and rejoin and follow the N13 for 5km. Take the D974 once again to Ste-Mère-l'Eglise (Point 7). Leave the village on the D974 and rejoin the N13. Leave the N13 on the D913 and after 1km turn right at the junction with the D974 into St-Côme-du-Mont (Point 8). Take the D974 from St-Côme-du-Mont into Carentan (Point 9). Continue on the D974 until the junction with the D544, 1km after crossing the canal on the exit from the town, and follow this road for 2.5km to the junction with the N174. Turn right and follow this road to Pont-Hébert (Point 10). Continue on the N174 to St-Lô (Point 11).

Leave St-Lô on the D974 and join the N174. After 4km leave the N174 and rejoin the D974 to Torigny-sur-Vire (Point 12). Leave Torigny-sur-Vire on the D13 and at La Lande-sur-Drôme turn left onto the D116. On reaching the D71 turn right for 200m and then left onto the D116 once again. At the junction with the D31 turn right onto the D31 to Cormolain (Point 13). Continue on the D31 to the junction with the D9. Follow the D9 past Maupertuis in the commune of St-Germain-d'Ectot to Fontenay-le-Pesnel (Point 14). Remain on the D9 to the junction with the D13. Turn right onto an unnumbered road and at the junction with the D173a turn left and follow this road into Cheux (Point 15). Take the D89 from Cheux to Tourville-sur-Odon. Turn left and follow the D675 into Caen (Points 16–30).

The Route on Foot and by Bike
This tour uses quite extensive lengths of footpath and canal towpaths as well as quiet tracks and roads. The terrain starts on the coastal plain of the Cotentin, climbs onto gently undulating terrain, crosses flat, marshland beyond Carentan and then once more enters undulating terrain before finishing on the flat land extending to Caen. The main tour covers 160km. Starting from Barfleur adds about 10km to the distance.

The Barfleur Variant
Leave Barfleur (Point 1) on the footpath *GRP Tour du Val de Sarre* which runs just to the east of the D902 through Montfarville (Point 2) and

follow the path to join the D902 just north of Anneville-en-Saire. The path is not well way-marked but is easy to follow.

> The path is initially on a paved surface, but just beyond Le Roches the surface changes to packed earth and becomes increasingly poor. There is a short section of paved road through Montfarville, but beyond the village the natural surface is poorly maintained with ruts, potholes and long grass. An alternative route for cyclists is to take the D902 from Barfleur to Anneville-en-Saire.

Continue on the *GRP Tour du Val de Sarre*, which follows the D902 for about 400m into Anneville-en-Saire and then turns right to follow an unnumbered road and two short stretches of track to La Pernelle (Point 3).

> The stretches of track of the *GRP Tour du Val de Sarre* after Le Petit Vicel and up the ridge to La Pernelle have natural surfaces which are rutted and muddy in wet weather. The alternative route for cyclists is to stay on the D902 and turn right to follow the D328 to La Pernelle.

From La Pernelle stay on the *GRP Tour du Val de Sarre* as far as the junction with the D125. Follow the D125 to the junction with the D26. Cross the D26 and follow footpaths and a short stretch of road to the church of St Vigor in Quettehou (Point 4). From the church descend to join the D902 and then the D1 through Quettehou to St-Vaast-la-Hougue (Point 5) and rejoin the main route.

> The track between La Pernelle to the D125 has a good natural surface, but an alternative for cyclists is to follow the D328 and then the D125. The path between the D26 and the church of St Vigor has a poor natural surface with long grass. An alternative route is to follow the D26 to the D902, turning right to follow the D902 until just south of the church. An unnumbered road leads to the church.

The Main Route
Leave St-Vaast-la-Hougue on the D1 initially and just to the west of the Hotel de la Granitière turn left to follow the Rue de Morsalines and join the *GR223* coastal footpath. It should be possible to follow the

path to Le Rivage and then take the D216E3 to join the D14. However, in the spring of 2014 the path was closed beyond Le Buissonet due to the path having been washed away by storms. If it has not been re-opened, take the D216E2 from Le Buissonet and turn left onto the D14. Follow this road to Morsalines.

The *GR223* between St-Vaast-la-Hougue and Le Buissonet is not suitable for cyclists: it is narrow, has sections with a stone surface which is slippery when wet and slopes towards the sea, and has low overhanging branches. Cyclists should take the D1 from St-Vaast-la-Hougue and turn left onto the D14 in Quettehou and follow this road to Morsalines.

From Morsalines take the D216 to St-Martin-d'Audouville. Join and follow the D62 to Valognes. Leave Valognes on the D974. On reaching a water tower on the left, 1km after the junction with the D2, turn left at La Victoire and follow an unnumbered road through La Croix Verte and Hameau Lesdos to join the D974 into Montebourg (Point 6).

The *GR223* runs from Montebourg to Ste-Mère-Eglise (Point 7). However, there are sections away from roads (from Joret to the D115, between Picard and the D115, and from Le Pont Percé to Ste-Mère-Eglise) which can be very difficult and even impassable in wet weather due to susceptibility to flooding and associated deep mud. A variety of alternative routes on roads can be used. One such route is to follow the D115 from Joganville through Emondeville to the junction with the D15 near Baudienville. The D15 is then followed into Ste-Mère-Eglise.

In addition to the difficulties with the *GR223* in wet weather described above, the section from Montebourg to just short of the D115 is rutted and potholed. Cyclists are advised to follow the D974 and D420 from Montebourg to Emondeville. Then follow the D115 to the junction with the D15 near Baudienville. The D15 is then followed into Ste-Mère-Eglise.

Leave Ste-Mère-Eglise on the D974. Near the junction with the N13 take the D67 through Ecoqueneauville and turn right to follow the D387. At Beaumont turn left and follow a track to the D129. Turn right and follow the D129. About 100m beyond the junction with the D329 carry straight on and follow an unnumbered road until 500m beyond La Vauxelle. Turn left onto the Rue des Planeurs and then right onto the D913. Cross over the N13 and follow unnumbered roads into St-Côme-du-Mont (Point 8).

> The section of track between Beaumont and the D129 has a poorly maintained natural surface. The alternative route for cyclists is to remain on the D67 until the junction with the D129 and rejoin the walking route after 1.5km.

From St-Côme-du-Mont follow the D974 through Carentan (Point 9). Immediately after crossing the river on leaving the town, turn right near a car wash to join the towpath alongside the river Taute and then the disused canal Vire et Taute. Leave the towpath and join the D89 near Le Port des Planques. After 800m join the D389. Follow the D389 to Le Dézert, with short sections on the D257 and D289 near Le Carrefour Vannier. Turn right onto the D8 in Le Dézert and then left onto the D257 which is followed to Pont-Hébert (Point 10).

> The towpath alongside the river and the disused canal is also initially a designated cycle path with a good surface. However, about 800m beyond the Maison des Ormes at the junction of the canal and the river, the path is on a grass surface. From here cyclists can take an unnumbered road which becomes the D444. Turn right at the junction with the D89 and rejoin the walking route near Le Port des Planques.

Leave Pont-Hébert on the N174. Just after crossing the railway, turn right and follow the D447 as far as Le Chasse Neuve. As the D447 turns sharply right go straight on and follow an unnumbered road to the junction with the N174. Cross the N174 and follow unnumbered roads running roughly parallel to the N174 into St-Lô (Point 11). From St-Lô take the D972 just beyond the chapel of La Madeleine and turn right onto the Rue des Noisetiers. Turn left at the Route Saint-Jean and then right onto the Rue Léon Jouhaux. Follow the D972 for 400m and then take the D11 to La Barre-de-Semilly. Leave the village on the D390 and go straight across the D59 to join the D90.

Follow the D90 to the junction with the D31 and follow this road through Cormolain (Point 13) to join the D9 just beyond Le Pont

Mulot. Stay on the D9 past Maupertuis through Fontenay-le-Pesnel (Point 14). On leaving the village turn right at the junction with the D13 onto an unnumbered road. Turn left onto the D173a and follow this road to Cheux (Point 15). Take the D89 out of the village and where the road turns sharply right through a right-angle after about 800m turn left and then almost immediately right to follow an unnumbered road which crosses over the A84. Take the first left after crossing over the motorway onto the D89a. Turn left at the junction with the D675 and follow this road into Caen (Points 16–30). Just beyond Verson the *GR221C* can be followed into Caen. This will add 2km to the tour.

> The *GR221C* from Verson runs on paved surfaces in places, but other sections are along earth paths which are often rutted and potholed. The alternative for cyclists is to remain on the D675.

What to See
Barfleur
Point 1: Barfleur is a pleasant fishing port but with little to show for its medieval past. The church of St Nicholas is the third on this spot. The

Medieval housing remaining in Barfleur in the Cour Ste Catherine. (Peter Hoskins)

original eleventh-century church was badly damaged by Edward III's troops in 1346 and, after having been restored, was finally destroyed during the sixteenth-century wars of religion. The only vestige of the medieval period in the town is a house in the Cour Ste Catherine just off Quai Henri Chardon (GPS 49.670018, -1.263726).

Montfarville
Point 2: There is no direct evidence that Montfarville was pillaged in 1346, but in view of its proximity to Barfleur and other villages which were attacked it seems highly probable that it did suffer alongside other settlements in the area. Two monuments contemporary to the time of the English invasion survive: the thirteenth-century bell-tower of the church of Notre-Dame in the Place du 8 Mai (GPS 49.654715, -1.269418) and a roadside cross dating from the late tenth or early eleventh century. The cross (400m north of the church near 9 Rue de la

The church of Notre-Dame in Montfarville. (Peter Hoskins)

The church of Ste Pétronille in La Pernelle. The bell-tower survived extensive damage in 1944. (Peter Hoskins)

Croix Muette, GPS 49.657386, -1.268792) was intended to protect travellers from brigands; presumably its powers did not extend to an English army.

La Pernelle
Point 3: The church of Ste Pétronille (GPS 49.618783, -1.298798) suffered extensive damage in the fighting around D-Day in 1944. The eleventh-century bell-tower was saved and restored. Next to the church is a small building built by the English as a guard-house in the fifteenth century.

Quettehou
Point 4: The church of St Vigor, where Edward III is said to have knighted the Black Prince and other young nobles after the landing, stands 500m to the west of the village in Rue St Vigor (GPS 49.591951, -1.309807). There is said to be a plaque inside the church commemorating the ceremony on 12 July 1346, but the church may not always be open.

The church of St Vigor in Quettehou. (Peter Hoskins)

St-Vaast-la-Hougue
Point 5: There are no surviving medieval buildings in St-Vaast, but this lively town with its busy marina is worth a visit to see the landing beaches (GPS 49.583403, -1.269067).

Montebourg
Point 6: Construction of the church of St Jacques (Place St Jacques, GPS 49.488193, -1.379488) started in 1318 and it was consecrated only seventeen years before the arrival of Edward III's army. It was badly damaged in 1944 but faithfully restored after the war. The abbey of Notre Dame de l'Etoile, just to the east of the D42 north of the town (GPS 49.491196, -1.375609), has been modernized and rebuilt over the centuries. It is said locally to have been taken and burnt by the English in 1346 and subsequently turned into a fortress. It was used by the

The abbey of Notre Dame de l'Etoile in Montebourg. (Peter Hoskins)

Duke of Lancaster as his headquarters in 1356 during the Black Prince's Poitiers campaign. It was not fortified, however, until 1357. The nineteenth-century abbey church is open to the public but the remainder of the building is used for a private *lycée*.

Ste-Mère-Eglise
Point 7: The village is famous for the unfortunate US paratrooper caught up on the church tower during the parachute drops on the eve of the D-Day landings, immortalized in the film *The Longest Day*. The transept of the church of Notre Dame de l'Assomption, on the D974 through the town (GPS 49.408329, -1.317368), dates from the twelfth century and parts of the nave and bell-tower from the early thirteenth century.

The church of Notre Dame de l'Assomption in Ste-Mère-Eglise. (Peter Hoskins)

The church of St Côme et St Damien in St-Côme-du-Mont. (Peter Hoskins)

St-Côme-du-Mont
Point 8: The twelfth-century church of St Côme et St Damien is in Rue des Ecoles (GPS 49.335461, -1.273044).

Carentan
Point 9: There is an arcade of surviving medieval houses, said to be the remains of a fourteenth-century covered market, in Place de la République (GPS 49.304510, -1.243934). The church of Notre Dame, Rue Esnouf (GPS 49.305626, -1.243760), was built in the eleventh century, but only the west door remains from the Romanesque period. It suffered serious damage during the Hundred Years War. Reconstruction started in 1443 during the English occupation.

Medieval arcaded building in Carentan, said to have been part of a fourteenth-century covered market. (Peter Hoskins)

The Romanesque west door of the church of Notre Dame in Pont-Hébert. (Peter Hoskins)

Pont-Hébert
Point 10: About 1.5km to the west of Pont-Hébert, just to the north of the D92 (GPS 49.171780, -1.158774), are the bell-tower and cemetery of the church of Notre Dame. The castle of Esglandes, where Edward III is said to have stayed on 21 July 1346, stood near here.

St-Lô
Point 11: The town suffered almost complete destruction during intense and protracted fighting between US and German forces during 1944 and those medieval monuments which survive have suffered a great deal and been extensively restored. There are extensive parts of the ramparts surviving, but only the Tour de la Poudrière in Place Général de Gaulle (GPS 49.116322, -1.091798) remains from the medieval period. The ramparts can be viewed from the Rue des Noyers below the tower (GPS 49.116322, -1.091798) and there are steps up to the tower and the ramparts. The church of Notre Dame, in Place Notre Dame (GPS 49.115336, -1.095068), was very badly damaged in 1944,

and the two spires which once graced the western façade were destroyed. However, elements of the medieval church, including the lower parts of the two towers at the western end of the nave, survived. The abbey church of Ste Croix, Place Ste Croix (GPS 49.116325, -1.085525), was originally built in the thirteenth century but restored in the nineteenth century and again following damage in 1944. Further outside the medieval town, but now well within the agglomeration, is the chapel of La Madeleine, once the chapel of a lepers' house. The chapel is just north of the D900, 200m west of the junction with the D88 (GPS 49.117182, -1.061245). Access by car is possible from the D88 and the Chemin de la Madeleine. Walkers or cyclists on the D900 can save a short distance by turning into the Rue de la Grange 200m west of the junction with the D88 and taking the path straight ahead as the Rue de la Grange swings left.

The Tour de la Poudrière in St-Lô, a surviving element of the medieval ramparts. (Peter Hoskins)

The gothic west door of the church of Notre Dame in St-Lô. (Peter Hoskins)

The chapel of La Madeleine in St-Lô. (Peter Hoskins)

Torigny-sur-Vire
Point 12: The thirteenth-century church of Notre Dame du Grand Vivier is in Rue Notre Dame (GPS 49.033547, -0.983282) and the twelfth-century church of St Laurent is in Rue Robert du Mont (GPS 49.034713, -0.980474).

Cormolain
Point 13: The bell-tower on the church of St André in Rue de la Drôme (GPS 49.129747, -0.854861) dates from the fourteenth century.

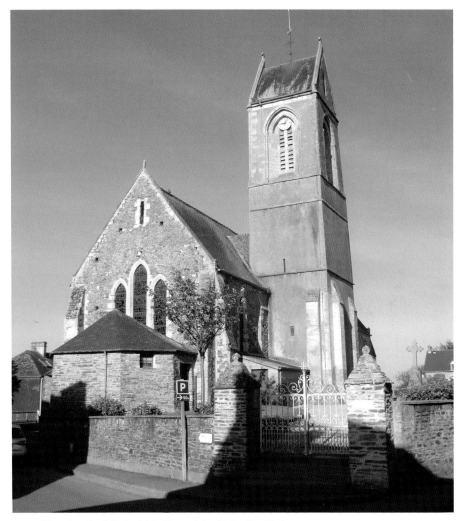

The church of St André in Cormolain. (Peter Hoskins)

Fontenay-le-Pesnel

Point 14: The army lodged in and around Fontenay-le-Pesnel on 25 July 1346 as it approached Caen. The church of St Aubin in Rue St Aubin (GPS 49.168362, -0.586132), somewhat confusingly in the suburb of St Martin, was built during the twelfth, thirteenth and fourteenth centuries. The fourteenth- and fifteenth-century church of St Martin has not fared so well, and having survived the centuries was largely destroyed in 1944. Only vestiges of the church tower remain near 26 Rue St Martin (the D9) (GPS 49.168362, -0.586132).

Remains of the church of St Martin in Fontenay-le-Pesnel. (Peter Hoskins)

The church of St Aubin in Fontenay-le-Pesnel. (Peter Hoskins)

Cheux

Point 15: The Black Prince lodged here before the advance on Caen on 25 July 1346. The church of St Vigor in the Rue des Dentellières (GPS 49.165007, -0.525252) was originally built in the twelfth and thirteenth centuries, modified in the nineteenth and restored after being damaged in 1944. The choir, transept and chapels are in the Romanesque style.

The church of St Vigor in Cheux, elements of which date back to the twelfth century. (Peter Hoskins)

Caen

Caen has a rich architectural heritage from the Middle Ages, despite having suffered extensively during the battle of Normandy in 1944.

Point 16: La Tour Guillaume le Roy, in the Boulevard des Alliées (GPS 49.184263, -0.359004) dates from the late fourteenth and fifteenth centuries and therefore post-dates the Crécy campaign. However, there is thought to have been an earlier tower here, one of two forming a gate for entry to the town from the river.

La Tour Guillaume le Roy. (Peter Hoskins)

Point 17: The Abbaye aux Hommes in the Esplanade Jean-Marie Louvel (GPS 49.181062, -0.371137) was founded in 1063. In 1346 it was defended with its own walls which were contiguous with those of the town. Guided visits are available throughout the year.

The Abbaye aux Hommes. (Peter Hoskins)

Point 18: Construction of the castle of Caen (GPS 49.185317, -0.361055), which resisted the army of Edward III in 1346, started in 1060. Extensive parts of the castle remain, including the parish church of St George which also dates from the eleventh century. An earlier church, long since abandoned for religious purposes and used in the nineteenth century as an arsenal, also survives, backing on to the walls of the citadel.

Point 19: The church of St Michel de Vaucelles, rue de l'Eglise-de-Vaucelles (GPS 49.174085, -0.355724), has a bell-tower surviving from the twelfth century. The remainder of the church dates from latter centuries. Vaucelles was outside the town in the fourteenth century and

*The castle of Caen.
(Peter Hoskins)*

*The Abbaye aux
Dames. (Peter
Hoskins)*

in theory was a distinct administrative entity but in reality was a suburb of the town.

Point 20: Also outside the town in 1346, and within the parish of Vaucelles, was the eleventh- and twelfth-century Chapelle de la Paix. A part of the chapel remains in rue du Marais (GPS 49.175470, -0.343008).

Point 21: The Abbaye aux Dames, Place Reine Matildhe (GPS 49.186801, -0.353372), was fortified in 1346 but stood outside and was separated from the town walls. It was originally consecrated in 1066. Free guided visits are available throughout most of the year.

Points 22 and 23: There are several houses reputed to be from the fourteenth century according to the French Ministry of Culture, but dated to later centuries by local sign boards. Two examples are the Hôtel du Quatrans, 25 rue de Geôle (GPS 49.184794, -0.362524), and 54 rue St Pierre (GPS 49.183399, -0.363283).

Fourteenth-century houses in Rue St Pierre. (Peter Hoskins)

The church of St Pierre in Caen. (Peter Hoskins)

Point 24: The church of St Pierre in Place St Pierre (GPS 49.183883, -0.360773), the construction of which started in the early fourteenth century, stood just inside the walls of the city.

Point 25: Built between the thirteenth and sixteenth centuries, the church of St Jean in Rue St Jean (GPS 49.180430, -0.358409) was at the heart of the undefended Île St-Jean.

Point 26: The church of St Etienne le Vieux, Rue Arcisse de Caumont (GPS 49.181127, -0.368891) was founded in the tenth century. It was repaired after the ravages of 1346 and from cannon fire from the tower of the Abbaye aux Hommes during Henry V's siege in 1417, but succumbed to damage in 1944 during the Battle of Normandy. The ruins that remain comprise elements from the thirteenth and fourteenth centuries and later.

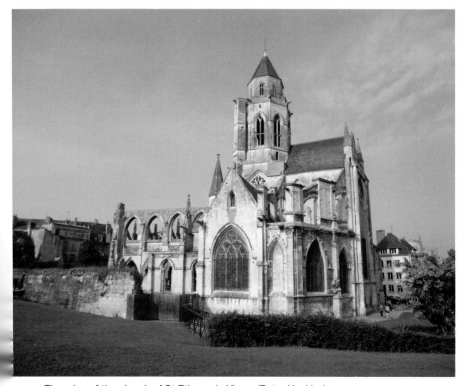

The ruins of the church of St Etienne le Vieux. (Peter Hoskins)

Point 27: The church of Notre Dame de Froide Rue in Rue St Pierre (GPS 49.182905, -0.364624) was within the walls of the fortified part of Caen. It dates in part from the thirteenth century.

Point 28: The church of St Nicholas in Rue St Nicholas (GPS 49.183879, -0.375664) was founded in 1083, shortly after the foundation of the nearby Abbaye aux Hommes.

Point 29: Just outside the defences of the town and the castle stands the thirteenth-century former collegiate church of St Sépulcre, founded in 1219 for ten canons, near 82 Avenue de la Libération (GPS 49.186786, -0.359543).

Point 30: Remains of the town walls can be seen in Les Fossés St Julien, close to the junction with the Rue Pémagnie (GPS 49.184314, -0.369250).

Vestiges of the town ramparts in Les Fossés St Julien. (Peter Hoskins)

Further Afield

St-Sauveur-le-Vicomte. There are substantial remains of the curtain walls and keep of the castle, the ancestral home of Godefroy d'Harcourt, in Rue Barbey d'Aurevilly (GPS 49.386014, -1.528543).

Maps

Maps at 1:25,000 and 1:100,000 scales		
Published by the *Institut National de l'Information Géographique et Forestière (IGN)* www.ign.fr		
Cartes de Randonnée – 1:25,000		
1310OT Cherbourg, Pointe de Barfleur	1313E St-Lô	1513O Aunay-sur-Odon
1311OT Valognes, Ste-Mère-Eglise, Utah Beach	1413O Torigni-sur-Vire	1512OT Bayeux
1312E Carentan	1413E Caumont-l'Eventé	1612OT Caen, Ouistreham (also Tour 2)
TOP 100 – 1:100,000		
TOP100106 Caen/Cherbourg-Octeville		

How to Get There and Back by Public Transport

Caen-Carpiquet and Paris airports are convenient for this tour. Caen-Carpiquet has a shuttle service to the city centre. All the Paris airports are well connected to the city centre for onward travel by rail. Ferries run from Portsmouth to Cherbourg and Caen-Ouistreham and from Poole to Cherbourg. Cherbourg ferry port is close to the town centre. Ouistreham is 18km from Caen city centre; there is a shuttle bus service but this does not operate during the evenings (www.twisto.fr). Railway services for this tour are provided by *SNCF Basse-Normandie Region*. The closest railway station to St-Vaast-la-Hougue is Valognes; there is a bus service provided by *Transports*

Manche (www.transports. manche.fr) with their *Express* service Line 13 between Valognes and Barfleur via St-Vaast-la-Hougue. Line 12 operates between Caen and Barfleur. Bicycles cannot be taken on these coaches; Valognes and Cherbourg are 20km and 28km respectively from St-Vaast-la-Hougue. Caen has a main-line railway station. Intermediate points on the tour with railway stations are Pont-Hébert, St-Lô and Carentan.

Where to Stay and Where to Eat
There are numerous places where refreshments can be found during the early part of the tour, although these become less frequent beyond St-Lô. Refreshments can be found in Barfleur, La Pernelle, Quettehou, St-Vaast-la-Hougue, Valognes, Montebourg, Ste-Mère-Eglise, Carentan, Pont-Hébert, St-Lô, Fontenay-le-Pesnel, Cheux, Verson and Caen. Surprisingly for a town with a population of more than 20,000, finding somewhere open in St-Lô on a Sunday morning very difficult. I was told later that the town was considered a 'dead' town by local French residents.

The local websites below give information on accommodation and refreshment for this tour:
www.ot-pointedesaire.com
www.ville-barfleur.fr
www.ot-cotentin-bocage-valognais.fr
www.saint-lo-agglo.fr
www.caen-tourisme.fr
www.normandie-tourisme.fr

Tour Two

Caen to Elbeuf

This tour covers the itinerary from the English departure from Caen on 31 July 1346 until the arrival at the first potential crossing point of the Seine at Elbeuf on 7 August. The tour covers a distance of 135km.

What Happened
The March to the Seine
Edward's army remained five days at Caen (Point 1), completing the plundering of the town but unable to capture the castle. There was time for rest and recovery from wounds, and some are said to have indulged in tourism, visiting the tomb of William the Conqueror and the female convent, the Abbaye aux Dames. The king and his council, however, made use of the pause to prepare for future operations. Edward's plan was to march east and cross the Seine between Rouen and Paris. Once across the river he then intended to turn north towards the river Somme. With the prospect of battle with the French,

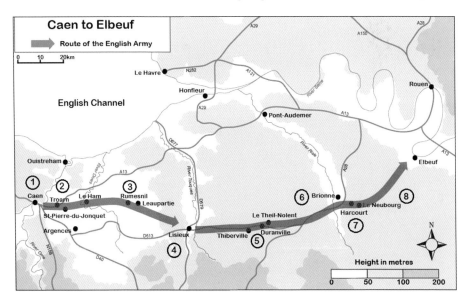

he had given orders for reinforcements to be sent to France: 1,200 archers were to be raised and 2,450 bows and 6,300 sheaves of arrows procured. Orders were given for 100 ships to be requisitioned to deliver the reinforcements and supplies by 20 August. The disembarkation port was to be Le Crotoy in the Somme estuary, about 120km north-east of Rouen and 200km north of Paris. Even in the worst case of a crossing of the Seine near Paris Edward could expect to reach Le Crotoy at about the planned date for the arrival of the reinforcements. Before Edward's departure from Caen around 300 prisoners, including the Count of Eu and the Lord of Tancarville, were shipped to England from the port of Ouistreham at the mouth of the Orne just north of Caen. Along with the prisoners went the English sick and the wounded unable to continue the march, plunder from Caen and St Lô and food taken during the march and surplus to requirements.

On Monday, 31 July Edward III's army was on the move again, probably with the objectives of an attack upon Rouen and bringing Philip to battle. However, a small force was left behind to continue with the siege of the castle in Caen. These unfortunate men were massacred during a sortie from the castle after the departure of the main body of the army. Although Edward could not know the fate of those he left behind, he had probably now abandoned any idea of retaining a base in Normandy, and as a consequence the policy of restraining the army was now discarded. From now on the army would, with official approval, rampage far and wide looting and burning a swathe of territory up to 60km wide on occasion.

The army advanced across wide open, flat countryside with a gentle climb onto a low ridge where Troarn (Point 2) stands, only 15km east of Caen. The Benedictine abbey at Troarn, of which the abbey church remains, was not fortified until 1359, at the time of another invasion by Edward III. Thus, although there was some resistance from the inhabitants of the abbey, this was quickly overcome and the town, which had been evacuated, was occupied. The king lodged here for the night. Argences, 8km south of Troarn, was reported to have been burnt.

The following day was again a short march, 18km, but this can be explained by the challenge of crossing the tidal salt marshes and river Dives with its many channels just to the east of Troarn. The army probably passed through the small settlements of St-Pierre-du-Jonquet and Le Ham during the crossing of the river, and stopped for

Marshland near the river Dives east of Troarn, which can be seen in the left background. (Peter Hoskins)

the night near Rumesnil (Point 3) and the nearby hamlet of Leaupartie.

On the Wednesday the army moved on to Lisieux (Point 4). The terrain now changes. The low-lying land that had been crossed since leaving Caen gives way to undulating hills rising 160m above the salt marshes of the Dives. It is not clear whether or not the rich town of Lisieux had walls at the time, but the cathedral close was walled and the bishop gave refuge to the town's inhabitants, who appear to have been left in peace by Edward's men. Perhaps they were content with the plunder in the deserted town.

Edward stayed at Lisieux for two nights, and on the Thursday two cardinals, the Italian Annibale Ceccano, Cardinal-Archbishop of Naples, and the Frenchman Étienne Aubert, Cardinal-Archbishop of Ostia, came to the king and pleaded with him to stop his advance. Ostensibly they came on behalf of Pope Clement VI, but they were really there at the behest of Philip. However, they had no authority to treat on behalf of the French king and nothing of substance to offer and were dismissed by Edward. On their arrival the cardinals had been robbed of twenty of their horses by Welsh troops and they had been forced to approach the king on foot. Before they left, their horses were restored to them.

On Friday, 4 August Edward's army left Lisieux in flames and resumed its march at a faster pace than hitherto since leaving Caen, covering 23km through Thiberville to Duranville (Point 5) and Le Theil-Nolent and then on Saturday, 5 August 34km through Brionne (Point 6) to Le Neubourg (Point 8). From Lisieux the army probably used the old Roman road to Brionne, which for much of the way is followed by the modern D613, and makes the most of the flat, open terrain before descending 100m into the valley of the Risle where the town stands.

Brionne was burned, as was the abbey of Bec-Hellouin 4km to the north. The army also passed through the village of Harcourt (Point 7), 6km south-east of Brionne, the ancestral home of Godefroy d'Harcourt's brother the Count of Harcourt, who was loyal to Philip. The route onwards to Le Neubourg starts with a steep climb out of the river valley, past the castle, which with the view from its dominant position would have given the town early warning of the approach of the English army, and onto gently rolling countryside. Le Neubourg was fortified but undefended and the English entered without opposition. Edward lodged in the castle, elements of which remain from the medieval period and which had an important place in the history of the English kings. Stephen had been proclaimed king here by the Norman barons following the death of Henry I in 1135, and twenty-five years later Henry II's son Henry the Young King was married to Marguerite of France in the abbey.

Sunday was a day of rest, but a detachment led by Godefroy d'Harcourt, and including Sir Thomas Holland in its number, set out to establish the situation at Rouen, which lies 40km north-east of Le Neubourg on one of the great swinging oxbow bends of the Seine. On the outskirts of Rouen lay the leper hospital of Petit-Quévilly and here they learned from an inmate that the French were present in force and that the bridge had been broken. As their reconnaissance continued they established that the town was well defended with King Philip present with the Counts of Harcourt and Dreux in his company. The suburbs south of the river, which included the monastery of Notre-Dame-du-Pré, had been abandoned with the inhabitants taking refuge in the medieval city on the right bank beyond the broken bridge. The detachment spread fire and destruction as far as the bridgehead on the left bank of the river and then returned to Le Neubourg, but not without suffering casualties, including the death of Sir John Daunay, a banneret of the Prince of Wales.

On Monday, 7 August the army was on the move again, this time to the north-east, almost certainly along the route of the modern D840, from Le Neubourg towards Elbeuf and the Seine 18km away. The going is initially easy, gradually descending towards the river with a final steep descent of 100m into the valley of the Seine from the high ground overlooking the town. Elbeuf lies on the south bank of the Seine with a bridge across the river. The Lord of Elbeuf was another member of the Harcourt family. He was with the French army and was to die at Crécy. The town itself was unprotected. In earlier times there had been a castle but this had been destroyed and not rebuilt by 1346. In addition, there were no walls or ditches, these being constructed later by the Duke of Bedford during the English occupation in the fifteenth century. However, the bridge had been broken and the north bank was defended by French troops. A party of Welshmen spotted some boats on the north bank and swam the river to seize them. They brought them back to the south bank and a raid was launched against the defended north end of the bridge which inflicted casualties on the defenders. Perhaps if sufficient men could have crossed the river the bridgehead could have been taken and held and the bridge repaired for the army as a whole to cross. In the event the raiders withdrew. Having failed to find a crossing at either Rouen or Elbeuf, the challenge now for Edward was to find somewhere else where he could cross to the right bank of the Seine.

The French Response

As Edward prepared to leave Caen towards the end of July, the French king was 140km to the east at Vernon. News reached Philip at around this time that the anticipated invasion from Flanders led by Hugh Hastings was about to start. He also received further bad news as the Duke of Normandy's attempt to take Aiguillon in Aquitaine went from bad to worse. Faced with challenges on three fronts, Philip seems to have had no clear plan. The Duke of Normandy remained in the south determined to save face if nothing else, while in the north on 29 July the king proclaimed the *arrière-ban* summoning all men of military age to assemble at Rouen and ordered the garrisoning of castles in Artois as a counter to Hastings' invasion. Genoese crossbowmen, having beached their galleys in the Seine, had also moved to Rouen. Men were gathering in the march of Flanders, Amiens and Paris, and others were leaving their homes to join the gathering French host.

The commander of the garrison in the castle at Caen, Robert Bertrand, was a resourceful and courageous man. As events elsewhere unfolded, he made a sortie from the castle, massacred the English troops left behind by Edward and then turned his attention to restoring French power in the Cotentin.

Philip was at Rouen around 31 July and initially moved slowly to the west towards Edward's advancing army. However, by 4 August Philip had changed his mind, and instead of intercepting the English he returned to Rouen, breaking the bridge over the Seine behind him. The plan now appears to have been to hold the English south of the river. A consequence of this course of action was that those living south of the Seine were left at the mercy of the marauding English army as it burnt and pillaged its way along the valley. The desperation of their situation is shown by the decision of the garrison commander of Pont-l'Évêque to release men from prison to man the ramparts.

The Route by Car

Leave Caen (Point 1) initially on the N814 towards the A13 *autoroute*. Do not join the A13 but turn north onto the D403 until the first roundabout. Follow the D675 to Troarn (Point 2) and then take the D78 through St-Pierre-du-Jonquet and Le Ham to the junction with the D49. Turn left onto the D49 and after 500m right onto the D117. Follow this road to Rumesnil (Point 3). Turn right in the centre of the village onto the D85 and then turn left onto the D85a after 800m. Stay on the D85a through St-Ouen-Le-Pin and cross the D59 onto the D151 which leads to Lisieux (Point 4).

Leave Lisieux on the D613. Follow the D613 through Duranville (Point 5), and at the intersection with the D438 turn left and follow this road to Brionne (Point 6). From Brionne take the D137 through Harcourt (Point 7) to Le Neubourg (Point 8). Follow the D840 from Le Neubourg to Elbeuf.

The Route on Foot and by Bike
The route is predominantly on quiet, minor roads with some short stretches on busier roads and with some paths and cycle tracks. The terrain varies, with some flat open countryside mixed from time to time with more undulating terrain.

In Caen (Point 1) join the footpath, the *GR36 – GR de Pays Tour du Bessin*, which runs along the north bank of the canal and is suitable for cyclists and pedestrians. Leave the path where the D226/D226a crosses the canal and follow the D226 to Sannerville. This road is initially busy, but after crossing the D513 after about 2km the road becomes much quieter. Much of the D226 has tracks or lanes reserved for cyclists and pedestrians. At a roadside cross in the centre of Sannerville carry straight on for 250m and turn left at the church. Follow this unnumbered road until you reach the D37. Turn right and follow this road into Troarn (Point 2).

> There is a short section of the D226, just after crossing the river Orne, which is signed as prohibited to cyclists travelling east. However, the path continues on the other side of the road and appears to be used in both directions.

From the centre of Troarn take the D675. Turn right after the church and walk past the abbey through modern housing along the Avenue de Chudleigh to the junction with the D78. Turn left and follow this road through St-Pierre-du-Jonquet and Le Ham to the junction with the D49 at the Carrefour Castelain. Take the D49 towards Beuvron-en-Auge, and after 600m turn right and follow the D117, which also coincides with the *GR de Pays Tour du Pays d'Auge* footpath, to Rumesnil (Point 3). At the crossroads in the centre of the village turn right onto the D85 and cross the D16. The chapel of St Gilles de Livet is 800m to the west along the D16. After crossing the D16 take the D85a after 800m and follow this road through St-Ouen-Le-Pin to the junction with the D59. Carry straight on and take the D151 to Lisieux (Point 4).

The most straightforward route from Lisieux to Brionne (Point 6) is to follow the course of the old Roman road, which is along the D613 for much of the way. However, the road is quite busy and the route proposed here for the most part avoids the D613 and passes further to the north. As a consequence it is slightly longer. Leave Lisieux on the

D613a. At the roundabout where the D613a meets the D613 turn right for 150m and turn left to follow the D510. Just beyond a roadside statue of the Virgin, 1.5km after joining the D510, fork right onto an unnumbered road. Up to this point the road can be busy, but from now on the route is much quieter. Follow this unnumbered road across the D510. Turn right after 600m to rejoin the D510 for 200m and then fork right to follow the D262. On reaching the junction with the D135, 500m before reaching the D613 at l'Hôtellerie, turn left and follow the D135/D157. Turn right onto the D707 through Les Places. Before reaching the D613 once again turn left onto an unnumbered road through La Haudardière and across the D22 onto the D695. On reaching a statue of the Virgin turn right onto an unnumbered road and take the first left onto a further unnumbered road. Turn right at the first junction and continue towards La Harèque. At the junction with the D28 turn left towards St-Aubin-de-Scellon. In St-Aubin turn right onto the D41. To visit Duranville (Point 5) stay on this road until the junction with the D613. To continue without visiting Duranville, turn left onto an unnumbered road through La Grande Rue to Le Theil-Nolent. Turn left in the village onto an unnumbered road. Take the second right to Bazoques. Cross the D834 and follow an unnumbered road across the D29 and through Boissy-Lamberville to the junction with the D43. Immediately before reaching the D613 turn left onto a track, initially grass surfaced, which follows the old Roman road. This track becomes an unnumbered road at the junction with the D31 and then after a further 1.5km the D701. Follow this road to the junction with the D438. Turn right and then take the first left into Brionne.

> The old Roman road from near the junction between the D43 and D613 has a grass surface with some potholes for the first 1km, followed by 400m of packed earth and stone. It is then paved for 400m to Le Chemin Chaussé. Beyond this the track consists of packed stone as far as a five-way junction with the D31. The remainder of the route to Brionne is paved. An alternative route for the cyclist is to leave the walker's route at La Vastine, turning left onto the D48. At the crossroads near Le Mailly and La Marotte turn left to continue on the D48. Take the next turning to the right and follow an unnumbered road past La Bruyère to rejoin the walker's route at the junction with the D31.

Leave Brionne on an unnumbered road, which runs parallel to and north of the D26, past the ruins of the castle. At the junction with the D137 take this route to Harcourt (Point 7). Leave the village to the north-east on the D156. Just beyond the Abbaye du Parc, at the bottom of the valley, turn right to follow a paved cycle path (*piste cyclable*). Follow the path to Pérouzette and then take an unnumbered road into Le Neubourg (Point 8).

The most straightforward route to Elbeuf is along the D840. However, the road is busy with traffic travelling fast. The last 1km into the town is dangerous for the walker, following a left-hand bend with no practicable refuge from traffic accelerating up the hill from Elbeuf. This road is not recommended, despite the savings in distance over the following route. Leave Le Neubourg on the D24. Follow this road to the junction with the D595 1km north of Cesseville. Turn left and follow an unnumbered road to Le Bec Thomas. Follow the D592 to the junction with the D86. Continue straight ahead, initially on an unnumbered road and then on the D26 and D7 to join the D144 to Elbeuf.

What to See

Caen
Point 1: *See* Tour One, pages 76–82.

Troarn
Point 2: The abbey church of St-Martin, Rue de l'Abbaye (GPS 49.181601, -0.177677) was founded in 1059 and William the Conqueror came to the abbey to confirm its charter in 1068. In addition to the damage done by Edward III's army in 1346, Troarn suffered under Henry V who confiscated lands belonging to the town and the abbey. Guided visits to the abbey can be arranged with the tourist office in the town: www.troarn.tourisme.free.fr, +33 2 31 39 14 22, office.troarn@wanadoo.fr.

Rumesnil
Point 3: The chapel of St-Gilles-de-Livet on the D16 (GPS 49.179443, 0.024495) south-west of the village dates from the eleventh century.

Lisieux
Point 4: The town suffered very heavy damage during the Battle of

The abbey church of St-Martin in Troarn. (Peter Hoskins)

The chapel of St-Gilles-de-Livet in Rumesnil. (Peter Hoskins)

Normandy in 1944, but several monuments from the Middle Ages survive. The cathedral of St-Pierre, Place François Mitterand (GPS 49.146413, 0.226022), was initially built in the twelfth century and the western façade dates from this period. There is also a fourteenth-century house, La Tour Carrée, 1 Rue Paul Baston (GPS 49.146746, 0.223938) and a perimeter tower, La Tour Lambert, on the line of the ramparts at 19 Quai des Remparts (GPS 49.145571, 0.221437), although this dates from the late fifteenth century.

The cathedral of St-Pierre in Lisieux. (Peter Hoskins)

La Tour Carrée in Lisieux. (Peter Hoskins)

La Tour Lambert in Lisieux. (Peter Hoskins)

Duranville
Point 5: The church in Duranville, on the south side of the D613 (GPS 49.149214, 0.509543), is remarkable for the twelfth-century west face and an ancient yew tree.

The west face of the church of St-Ouen in Duranville. (Peter Hoskins)

Brionne

Point 6: The church of St-Martin, Place de l'Eglise (GPS 49.195271, 0.719199), was originally constructed in the eleventh century. It was largely rebuilt in the fifteenth century although elements, notably the nave, remain from the thirteenth century. The ruins of the eleventh-century castle keep stand on the high ground to the east of the town (GPS 49.195192, 0.723022). The ruins can be reached along the Sentier du Vieux Château. The castle walls were 4.5m thick at the base tapering to 3m at the top. The keep had a balcony which could hold 100 men-at-arms.

The ruins of the castle keep of Brionne. (Peter Hoskins)

Harcourt
Point 7: Château Harcourt, 7km north of the village of Harcourt (GPS 49.173370, 0.787009), the twelfth- and fourteenth-century seat of the Harcourt family, is open to the public: www.harcourt-normandie.fr.

Le Neubourg
Point 8: The most notable monument here is part of the castle. The keep, chapel and walls were demolished in the late eighteenth century and only part of the living quarters remains. The building stands in the Place du Château (GPS 49.148272, 0.900111), but a view from the north along the Rue des Remparts (GPS 49.149549, 0.898083), although partly obscured by trees, gives a better impression of the defensive features of the castle. The church of Notre-Dame in the Rue de la République (GPS 49.149026, 0.902686), with its thirteenth-century choir, and the thirteenth-century chapel of St-Jean at 8 Rue de Verdun (GPS 49.150984, 0.907018) also survive.

The castle of Le Neubourg seen from the Place du Château. (Peter Hoskins)

Further Afield

Not directly on the itinerary of Edward III's army, but important to events during the campaign, is Rouen. Among the many monuments to be seen in Rouen are the cathedral in Place de la Cathédrale (GPS 49.440377, 1.09422), the site of Joan of Arc's execution in the Place du Vieux Marché (GPS 49.443052, 1.088396), and the keep of the castle, La Tour Jeanne d'Arc, in Rue du Donjon (GPS 49.44647, 1.094393), where she was held during her trial. The Rouen tourism website has detailed information on museums and architectural monuments: www.rouentourisme.com.

The keep of Rouen castle, now known as La Tour Jeanne d'Arc. (Peter Hoskins)

Maps

Maps at 1:25,000 and 1:100,000 scales		
Published by the *Institut National de l'Information Géographique et Forestière (IGN)* www.ign.fr		
Cartes de Randonnée – 1:25,000		
1612OT Caen, Ouistreham (also Tour 1)	1712E Lisieux	1912O Bourgtheroulde-Infreville
1612E Dives-sur-Mer	1812O Cormeilles	1912E Elbeuf
1712O Cambremer	1812E Brionne	
TOP 100 – 1:100,000		
TOP100117 Caen/Evreux (also Tour 3)		

How to Get There and Back by Public Transport

Caen-Carpiquet and Paris airports are convenient for this tour. Caen-Carpiquet has a shuttle service to the city centre. All the Paris airports are well connected to the city centre for onward travel by rail. Ferries run from Portsmouth to Caen-Ouistreham which is 18km from Caen city centre. There is a bus service between the port and Caen (www.twisto.fr) but this does not operate during the evenings. Railway services for this tour are provided by *SNCF* Basse-Normandie and Haute-Normandie Regions. Caen has a main-line railway station. Regional trains from the Haute-Normandie Region provide a service from Brionne and Elbeuf-St-Aubin to Oissel for main-line trains to Paris. Main-line trains also serve Lisieux. There is a bus service between Caen and Troarn (www.busverts.fr).

Where to Stay and Where to Eat

There are numerous places to eat and drink on this tour, sometimes in even small villages. Refreshments can be found at Caen, Colombelles,

Troarn, Beuvron-en-Auge, Le Pré-d'Auge, Lisieux, La Croix-de-Pierre, Ouilly-du-Houley, L'Hôtellerie, Thiberville, Duranville, Brionne, Iville, Fouqueville and Elbeuf.

The local websites below give information on accommodation and refreshments for this tour:

www.caen-tourisme.fr

www.normandie-tourisme.fr

www.lisieux-tourisme.com

www.troarn.tourisme.free.fr

www.argences.com

www.leneubourg.fr

www.rouentourisme.com

Tour Three
Elbeuf to Poissy

This tour covers the itinerary from the English departure from Elbeuf on 8 August 1346 until the crossing of the Seine at Poissy on 16 August. The tour covers a distance of 122km.

What Happened
The March along the Seine

Having failed to find a crossing at either Rouen or Elbeuf, the challenge now for Edward was to find somewhere else where he could cross to the right bank of the Seine. Between Elbeuf and Paris the main bridges were at Pont-de-l'Arche, Vernon, Mantes-la-Jolie, Meulan-en-Yvelines, Poissy and St-Cloud. A little over 2km to the east of Elbeuf there is a confluence of the rivers Seine and Eure. The Eure is a minor obstacle compared with the Seine, but for the next 10km it runs parallel to the Seine, with the two rivers separated by a narrow strip of land. It is only beyond Pont-de-l'Arche that the rivers start to diverge.

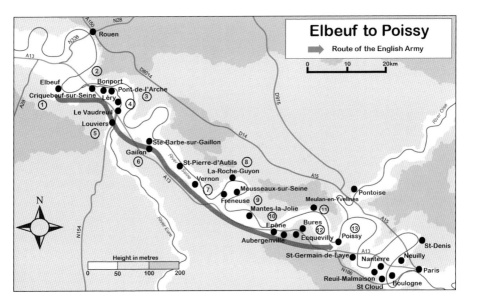

At some point the Eure needs to be crossed if the Seine is to be followed. Judging by the itinerary of Edward's army this crossing was made at or near Louviers. The first bridge over the Seine reached after leaving Elbeuf was, and still is, at Pont-de-l'Arche, which, in common with Vernon and Mantes-la-Jolie, was a walled town on the left bank of the river. It could be reinforced at will from the north provided the French held the bridge.

On Tuesday, 8 August the army passed through Criquebeuf-sur-Seine (Point 1) and past the twelfth-century abbey of Bonport (Point 2) close to the river Eure, and tried to storm the walls of Pont-de-l'Arche (Point 3). However, the town was very well protected with walls on all sides, including close up to the river Eure, and a castle within the town which would also have to be taken to gain access to the bridge. This would have been a tough nut to crack, and the local garrison under the command of Jean du Bosq, a royal official, held the English off long enough for elements of the main body of the French army to arrive and the assault was abandoned. While at Pont-de-l'Arche Edward received a message from Philip challenging him to settle their dispute by personal combat. The code of chivalry viewed refusal of such a challenge as dishonourable, but this was no more than political manoeuvring and, just as Philip had refused a similar challenge from Edward in 1340, the challenge was rejected with the response that the two kings would meet in battle at Paris. The English assault on Pont-de-l'Arche having been repulsed, the army moved on to lodge in the vicinity of Léry (Point 4) and Le Vaudreuil that night. As they went, the men continued to destroy, burn and loot across a wide band of territory.

The next day, Wednesday, 9 August, the English burned Le Vaudreuil and then pressed on to the next bridge at Vernon, passing through and burning Louviers (Point 5), a rich town noted for its cloth trade. Louviers was not walled, work only starting on defences twenty years later, and as a consequence it had probably been abandoned as the English approached. Having crossed the Eure in the vicinity of Louviers, there was a steady climb of 150m before the English came to Gaillon (Point 6) and the nearby village of Ste-Barbe-sur-Gaillon, standing on high ground, before a descent into the Seine valley. Both were looted and burnt but not before some fierce fighting in Gaillon, which was garrisoned with a castle standing on high ground in the north of the town. An unsuccessful assault on a castle on the Seine was recorded, possibly the one in Gaillon, which resulted in both Sir Thomas Holland and Sir Richard Talbot being wounded. An attempt by the town garrison of Gaillon to withdraw towards Vernon (Point 7) through the east gate turned into a rout with the English pursuing and cutting down the fleeing French.

Close to Vernon the English stormed and burned the unprotected village of Longueville, now the village of St-Pierre-d'Autils, and stormed its castle. Nothing remains of a castle here and it may be that this was a fort 4km to the north, known as Boute-Avant or Le Goulet, built by Richard the Lionheart and destroyed on the orders of Henry V in 1422, on the Île-des-Boeufs in the Seine. They massacred the garrison of the castle. The bridge at Vernon was well defended. It would have been necessary to take the town to gain access to the bridge, which was itself fortified. The bridge was constructed largely of stone but with a wooden section that could easily be destroyed, and passed through the castle of the Château des Tourelles at the eastern end, standing in the Seine with marsh behind. This was all too much for Edward's men and they could get no further than the suburbs, which were fired along with the surrounding countryside.

During the next days the search for a crossing continued. On several stretches of the Seine from just downstream of Vernon until Poissy the left bank of the river runs close to high ground, with only a narrow strip of land in the valley suitable for movement. It is probable that for much of the march from the vicinity of Vernon to Poissy the bulk of the army took routes across the higher ground, with scouts staying in the river valley to reconnoitre potential crossing places. This would also have given the army the advantage of a more direct route, rather than following the sinuous course of the river.

On Thursday, 10 August the king stopped for the night at Freneuse and the prince's division 3km further east at Mousseaux-sur-Seine. The formidable castle of La-Roche-Guyon (Point 8) is visible from the high ground 1.5km south of Freneuse. It must have looked a tempting target 7km away to the north-east, and on the same day a detachment under the command of Robert de Ferrers courageously crossed the river with a few men in a rowing boat and took the fortress. This was a quite remarkable feat since the castle, with two concentric outer walls, ditches and a keep on high ground had a reputation for being

The Seine, 3km upstream from Vernon, viewed from the right bank. The river runs close up against the hills and the bulk of the army would probably have passed across this higher ground with scouts following the river. (Peter Hoskins)

very strong. The garrison commander had clearly misjudged the situation and, thinking that he was under attack by the whole English army, surrendered both the castle and his men. Some forty or so French knights were killed or captured, although among the English Sir Edward Bois was killed by a stone thrown by the defenders. Having secured the word of his prisoners to pay ransoms in due course, de Ferrers returned to the safety of the other bank. It was while Edward rested at Freneuse that the cardinals came back to treat with the king once more. However, although this time they came openly from the French king, the terms on offer had not been improved and the discussions were fruitless.

On Friday, 11 August the army pressed on to Mantes-la-Jolie (Point 9), now flying red banners symbolizing immediate readiness to give battle and fight to the death, but, finding several thousand French troops drawn up under the wall, passed on without attempting to take either the town or the bridge. Between Mantes-la-Jolie and Poissy the left bank of the river lies hard up against a steep escarpment in a number of places, and the itinerary of the army, with a stop for the Friday night at pône (Point 10) and Aubergenville and on the following night at Equevilly and Bures indicates that the major part of the army crossed the higher ground rather than attempting to follow the river.

During the day the army had passed by Meulan-en-Yvelines (Point 11), where almost seventy-five years later Henry V was to set eyes for the first time on his future wife Catherine de Valois, daughter of Charles VI of France. The Earls of Warwick and Northampton had approached the town, which unlike Pont-de-l'Arche, Vernon and Mantes-la-Jolie, lay to the north of the river. There is an island in the middle of the Seine, which was strongly fortified. The bridge was in fact in two parts: the first linking the south bank, defended by a barbican, to the island and the second crossing from the island to the town. This would have been a difficult bridge to take, but to compound the problem the north end had been broken. Having been abused by the defenders of the barbican the English withdrew, but not until they had destroyed the suburb of Les Mureaux.

On Sunday, 13 August Edward came to Poissy (Point 13) and occupied the town, along with St-Germain-en-Laye with its royal hunting lodge. The English were now only 20km from Paris. Both Poissy and St-Germain-en-Laye had been abandoned, and the bridge over the Seine at Poissy had been broken. The king lodged in a new mansion built for Philip while the Black Prince settled into the old palace nearby. The French seem to have relied on the destruction of the bridge as sufficient defence, but they had not reckoned on the carpenters with Edward's army. The English immediately set about rebuilding the bridge and later that day an initial span had been made with a 20m tree. The French received the news with disbelief, but men on the way from Amiens led by two minor barons, the Lords of Aufremont and Revel, were diverted to investigate. By the time they arrived it was too late and they found that the first of the English were already across the river. However, they were few in number and there was a risk of the French retaking possession of the north bank. Seeing the danger the constable, the Earl of Northampton, courageously led several hundred men across the perilous single span, only some 30cm wide, and by the time Aufremont and Revel were able to launch an attack the English bridgehead was well defended. The French were driven off, with perhaps 200 killed. In their haste to escape, the retreating French rode off two or three each astride un-harnessed cart horses, leaving behind twenty-one carts loaded with stone shot and crossbow quarrels and provisions. The carts were emptied and then burnt. Meanwhile the English continued to consolidate their position and to construct the replacement bridge. By the next morning a bridge capable of bearing carts was in place. There were no further serious attempts by the French to prevent the crossing of the army and on Wednesday, 16 August Edward started to move north towards the Somme. By the time he did so, the western outlying Parisian settlements of Nanterre, Rueil (now part of Rueil-Malmaison), Neuilly, Boulogne and St-Cloud had all been reduced to ashes.

The French Response
As Edward continued his march towards the Seine, the cardinals who had come to him at Lisieux were pressing Philip to offer terms which might secure peace. He agreed to restore the County of Ponthieu and lost territories in Aquitaine, and also offered a marriage alliance between the two crowns. However, the sting in the tail was that Philip still required homage from Edward for his lands held in France. The cardinals set out to meet Edward, accompanied by a French archbishop, to deliver Philip's terms, but they were not optimistic of success. They also said that they did not believe that Philip was likely to make any further concessions. Edward sent them on their way saying that he would respond in due course, but that he would not delay his march while discussing the terms. In the event Edward moved north without attempting to engage Philip.

Philip now decided to concentrate his forces against Edward's army with the objective of holding the English at the Seine. The troops at Amiens intended to counter Hugh Hastings were now called to join Philip, leaving only small detachments, and the Duke of Normandy was finally overruled and his army recalled to join the king, although the duke wasted valuable time before departing for the north trying to negotiate a truce in the south-west with the Earl of Lancaster.

When on Sunday, 13 August the English reached Poissy and St-Germain-en-Laye, they were within striking distance of Paris, and there was great alarm in the capital, and 500 men-at-arms of Jean de Luxembourg, King of Bohemia, were deployed in the streets to maintain order. Barricades were constructed, stores of missiles were gathered and preparations made to destroy suburbs outside the walls to deny them to the English. The French army was now substantial, with perhaps 8,000 men-at-arms, 6,000 Genoese and a large number of infantry. However, Philip faced a problem with their deployment. He could not defend Paris effectively without splitting his army, with the risk that entailed of one part being engaged by the whole of the English army. The bends in the river compounded his problems when it came to defending the bridges at Poissy and St-Cloud. To the north the distance between the two was around 60km, while the English only had to cover around a third of this distance. In addition, the walls of Poissy were in poor repair, making the defence of the town and the bridge even more problematic. Thus, he had abandoned the bridge at Poissy and concentrated his forces at St-Cloud, with his headquarters 15km further north in the abbey of St-Denis. On learning that the English were crossing at Poissy, Philip might have been expected to either advance from the north to counter the crossing or to cross the river himself and attack Edward from the south as he was engaged in crossing the river. He did neither. Instead he broke the bridge at St-Cloud and withdrew further north between St-Denis and Paris. The citizens of Paris could see the smoke rising from the fires in St-Cloud and St-Germain-en-Laye, as well as numerous hamlets and villages to the south of the capital.

While Edward was at Poissy, Philip, on 14 August, sent a message to challenge Edward to battle between 17 and 22 August. Two sites were proposed: one close to and south of Paris and another near Pointoise, 15km north of Poissy. In the event the challenge did not reach Edward before his departure from Poissy. However, Philip seems to have anticipated that he would have battle with the English at the first site since on Tuesday, 15 August he moved his army through Paris and towards the chosen battleground. The next day Edward was on the march away from Philip, heading to the Somme. Meanwhile, Philip was paying the price for drawing troops away from the forces originally intended to defend against the incursion of Hugh Hastings, and as Philip manoeuvred near Paris, Hastings and his Flemings were spreading destruction in the north.

The Route by Car

Leave Elbeuf on the D921 and follow this road through Criquebeuf-sur-Seine (Point 1) to Pont-de-l'Arche (Point 3). Bonport Abbey (Point 2) can be reached from the D921 near Pont-de-l'Arche. Take the D77 from Pont-de-l'Arche, and 1km after the junction with the D77e fork left onto an unnumbered road into Léry (Point 4). Leave the village towards Val-de-Reuil to rejoin the D77. At the junction with the D313 1km beyond Le Vaudreuil, turn right to follow the D313 into Louviers (Point 5). Leave Louviers on the D6155, turn right onto the D6015 near Heudebouville and follow this road through Gaillon (Point 6) to Vernon (Point 7). Now take the D915 to Bonnières-sur-Seine and then the D113 through Mantes-la-Jolie (Point 9). To visit La-Roche-Guyon (Point 8), turn left in Bonnières-sur-Seine and follow the D100 to the village. To rejoin the main route either retrace the route to Bonnières or continue on the D100 to join the D147 at Vétheuil and follow this road to Mantes-la-Jolie. After leaving Mantes, in Mézières-sur-Seine fork right and follow the D130 into Épône (Point 10). Leave the village on the D139 and rejoin the D113 through Ecquevilly (Point 12). To visit Meulan-en-Yvelines (Point 11) leave the D113 near Aubergenville and follow the D19 to Meulan. Return to the main route on the D43 at Equevilly. Rejoin and follow the D113 to the junction with the D153 near Orgeval. Follow the D153 into Poissy (Point 13).

The Route on Foot and by Bike
This tour is more or less along the valley of the Seine. There are stretches on quiet tracks and minor roads but there are extensive sections on quite busy D roads. There are often alternatives to these sections of busy road but at the expense of significant additions to distance. Some of the towns sprawl over a wide area and the route cannot avoid some drab, modern suburbs.

Leave Elbeuf on the footpath/cycle track which runs between the Seine and the D921. The path stays close to the river and diverges from the D921 about 1.5km after the road bridge over the Seine in Elbeuf. Stay on the path and, after a further 1km, follow an unnumbered road through Criquebeuf-sur-Seine (Point 1) to the junction with the D321. Follow the D321 and D77 past the abbey of Bonport (Point 2) into Pont-de-l'Arche (Point 3). Leave the town on the D77. A little over 1km after the roundabout with the D6015 at some traffic lights, just before a cemetery on the left, turn right to follow the *Voie Impériale* signposted forest track. After about 1.5km the track crosses the way-marked *GR222A*. After a further 400m turn left to follow a grass track across the D77 into Léry (Point 4). Make your way out of Léry on the Rue de Verdun and Route des Lacs to rejoin the D77.

The *Voie Impériale* has a well-maintained natural surface of packed earth and stone, with some loose stones. However, after the left turn to descend into Léry the condition of the path deteriorates markedly. The surface is grass, and muddy and potholed. The path also descends steeply in places. The forest track beyond the left turn on the walker's route, now the *Voie Blanche*, appears to have a good surface, but an alternative route for cyclists is to remain on the D77 between Pont-de-l'Arche and Léry.

Follow the D77 through Le Vaudreuil. Immediately after crossing a disused railway line turn right onto the D313 and follow this road into Louviers (Point 5). From Louviers there is no choice but to follow the relatively busy D6155 and then the D6015 to Heudebouville. A little over 1km after the junction of the D6155 and D6015, fork right and follow the D177 and rejoin the D6015 in Ste-Barbe-sur-Gaillon. After 600m fork left and follow the road into Gaillon (Point 6). Leave the town on the D77. There is now a choice: either follow the relatively busy D6015 or take unnumbered roads to the south through Angreville, Habloville and Bailly to rejoin the D6015 near Le Goulet. Follow the D6015 and turn right onto the D73 near St-Pierre-d'Autils. Follow the D73, D527, Rue Jules Ferry, Rue Grégoire, Boulevard de Gaulle, Boulevard Jean Jaurès and D64 into Vernon (Point 7). It is possible to remain clear of the D6015 by turning south on unnumbered roads in Bailly and routing via St-Étienne-sous-Bailleul to rejoin the route at St-Pierre-d'Autils, but this adds considerably to the distance.

From Vernon cross the Seine on the D161, and in Vernonnet turn right to follow the D5 through Giverny and then right onto the D201. There are stretches of footpath parallel to the D5 which can be used. Follow the D201 through Bennecourt and across the Seine to join the D113 in Bonnières-sur-Seine. There are paths away from the D113, but they add significantly to the distance. The D113 is relatively busy, but for most of its length to Rosny-sur-Seine there are either wide verges or parallel paths. Through Rosny-sur-Seine there is a good track for cycles and pedestrians. On approaching the hospital complex on the left, turn left and follow Boulevard Sully. Turn right to follow the Rue Nungesser et Coli, continue straight on along the Rue du Dr Bretonneau, left into Avenue Albert Camus, and right into Rue des

Garennes to Gassicourt. Turn left into Rue du Val de Seine, right into Rue Maurice Braunstein and then follow the Rue des Écoles into Mantes-la-Jolie (Point 9).

South-east of Mantes-la-Jolie there is a veritable spaghetti junction of busy roads. The quietest route out is along the river on the Quai des Cordeliers, and then, having passed under the D983, follow the Rue de la Tuilerie and the Allée de Chantereine to the junction with the D983. Immediately turn left onto a path which leads to the D113. This is a potentially busy road but it does at least have the benefit of wide cycle- and footpaths along the side. Follow the D113 to Mézières-sur-Seine. Fork right onto Rue Nationale a little more than 2km after crossing under the motorway and continue into Épône (Point 10). It is possible for the walker to avoid much of the D113 by turning right onto the D158 800m after joining the D113 on leaving Mantes-la-Jolie and then following unnumbered roads and the *GR26* footpath through La Villeneuve to Épône.

> The *GR26* is not recommended for cyclists. The alternative to the D113 is to follow the D158 from the D113 through Boinville-en-Mantois and then to take the D139 into Épône.

Rejoin the D113 to the east of Épône. Follow this road to Ecquevilly (Point 12) and then on past Orgeval to the junction with the D153. Turn left and follow the D153 into Poissy (Point 13). The D113 is not a pleasant road to walk, but there are wide verges and paths and it can be used on foot with caution. There are alternatives from Épône via Ecquevilly, using minor roads and the *GR26* but they involve substantial deviations from the direct route with consequent increases in distance.

> The *GR26* is not recommended for cyclists and it is impossible to avoid the D113 entirely between Épône and Ecquevilly and Ecquevilly and Poissy. The best alternative is to take the D113 initially from Épône and then just beyond Aubergenville follow the D14 and D19 to Flins-sur-Seine. Then follow unnumbered roads to rejoin the D113 about 1km to the west of Ecquevilly. Beyond Ecquevilly follow unnumbered roads via Morainvilliers, Montamets and Orgeval. Then rejoin the main route on the D153 into Poissy.

The church of Notre Dame in Criquebeuf-sur-Seine. (Peter Hoskins)

What to See
Criquebeuf-sur-Seine
Point 1: The bell-tower of the church of Notre Dame in the Rue du Pont des Alliés (GPS 49.306008, 1.097852) dates from the fourteenth century.

Bonport Abbey

Point 2: The English army passed the abbey of Bonport on the approach to Pont-de-l'Arche. According to legend, this Cistercian abbey was founded by Richard the Lionheart in 1189 in thanks for his safe arrival on the river bank after getting into danger pursuing a deer. The church was destroyed during the French revolution but many of the monastery buildings remain. It is open to the public between April and September during the afternoons on Sundays and public holidays, and in July and August every afternoon except Saturday: www.abbayedebonport.com, Rue du Générale de Gaulle, Pont-de-l'Arche (GPS 49.306016, 1.140395).

Bonport Abbey. (Peter Hoskins)

Pont-de-l'Arche

Point 3: There are a number of vestiges of the defences of the town. The Tour de Crosne, private property but visible from Quai Maréchal Foch (GPS 49.306088, 1.153502), has a thirteenth-century base with the upper part having been restored by the architect Viollet le Duc in the nineteenth century. The towers of Tour St-Vigor and the Presbytère are also visible from the Quai Maréchal Foch (GPS 49.305945, 1.154693 and 49.305814, 1.155573). Parts of the gate at the Port de Crosne in Rue

The Tour St-Vigor on the ramparts of Pont-de-l'Arche. (Peter Hoskins)

de Crosne (GPS 49.305004, 1.153532), and the well-preserved Tour de Bailliage near the Place du Souvenir (GPS 49.304345, 1.153766) also survive.

Léry
Point 4: The church of St-Ouen is in Place de l'Église (GPS 49.285740, 1.209400) with elements from the eleventh and twelfth centuries.

Louviers
Point 5: The church of Notre Dame in rue Pierre Mendes France (GPS 49.212906, 1.169671) has some minor elements from the eleventh to

The church of St-Ouen in Léry. (Peter Hoskins)

The church of Notre Dame in Louviers. (Peter Hoskins)

thirteenth centuries, but its most notable feature is the bell-tower, of a distinctly military character, built later in the Hundred Years War in 1414.

Gaillon
Point 6: The present château in Gaillon, in the Allée du Château (GPS 49.160839, 1.329999), was built on the site of the earlier castle in the sixteenth century. Its dominant position above the town is evident. It is open between April and October, see the town website (www.ville-gaillon.fr) for opening hours.

The château of Gaillon. (Peter Hoskins)

Vernon

Point 7: Vernon has a number of medieval buildings, including the collegiate church of Notre Dame in Rue Carnot (GPS 49.093274, 1.485931), the twelfth-century castle keep, the Tour des Archives in Rue des Écuries des Gardes (GPS 49.093826,1.484151), and numerous domestic buildings with Rue Potard (GPS 49.093956,1.484983) having fine examples of half-timbered buildings: see www.vernon27.fr/ Decouvrir-Vernon. In Vernonnet, on the right bank of the Seine and close to the modern bridge (GPS 49.097982, 1.489200), stands the Château des Tourelles and the remains of the old bridge, together with a mill. The château is thought to have been constructed by King Henry II.

La Tour des Archives in Vernon, formerly the keep of the castle. (Peter Hoskins)

The remains of the medieval bridge at Vernon in the suburb of Vernonnet. (Peter Hoskins)

Vernon, Château des Tourelles in the suburb of Vernonnet. (Peter Hoskins)

La-Roche-Guyon

Point 8: A renaissance château (GPS 49.080985, 1.628575) now takes pride of place, but the keep of the twelfth-century fortress still stands. The château is open throughout the year. Opening hours vary considerably with the season: www.chateaudelarocheguyon.fr.

Mantes-la-Jolie

Point 9: There are numerous buildings in Mantes-la-Jolie surviving from the Middle Ages. The priory church of Ste-Anne de Grassicourt in the Impasse de Ste-Anne (GPS 49.002271, 1.697850), 2km north-west of the town centre, would have been outside the town walls. Within the walls were the church of St Maclou, of which only the tower survives in the Place du Marché au Blé (GPS 48.991038, 1.717328), and the collegiate church of Notre-Dame in Place de l'Étape (GPS 48.990532, 1.719480). The medieval walls and gates of the town were improved substantially twice during the Hundred Years War, between 1365 and 1373 and again between 1419 and 1449 under the English occupation. There are several elements of these medieval fortifications which survive: the Port du Prêtre (GPS 48.990055, 1.721755) and a

The priory church of Ste-Anne de Grassicourt in the suburbs of Mantes-la-Jolie. The nave was restored after damage in 1944. (Peter Hoskins)

The twelfth- and thirteenth-century collegiate church of Notre Dame. (Peter Hoskins)

A surviving gate in Mantes-la-Jolie, named the Port du Prêtre in memory of an attempt by a priest to retake the town from the English in 1421. The gate appears lower than it would have been in the Middle Ages, having lost some height with the construction of quays along the river in the nineteenth century. (Peter Hoskins)

The perimeter tower of St-Martin. (Peter Hoskins)

watch tower and a stretch of wall (GPS 48.990055, 1.721755) in the Quai des Cordeliers, a length of wall below the site of the castle in the Rue des Tanneries (GPS 48.989411, 1.721774), a tower, the Tour St-Martin, in the Rue des Martraits (GPS 48.987048, 1.718701), and the site and footings of the gate known as the Chant à l'Oie in the Rue Porte Chant à l'Oie (GPS 48.992484, 1.715910).

Épône
Point 10: The church of St Béat in the Place des Fêtes (GPS 48.955399, 1.813884), although restored extensively in the nineteenth century, dates from the eleventh, twelfth and thirteenth centuries.

The church of St Béat in Épône. (Peter Hoskins)

Meulan-en-Yvelines

Point 11: Meulan is predominantly to the north of the Seine. The medieval bridge passed across an island, with the northern part known as the Petit Pont and the southern section as the Grand Pont. The northern section, also known as the Pont aux Perches, survives (GPS 49.004061, 1.910006). The church of St Nicholas, with elements from the twelfth century, is in Rue de la Côté St Nicholas (GPS 49.006318, 1.907843).

Ecquevilly

Point 12: The church of St Martin, restored over the centuries but

The church of St Martin in Ecquevilly. (Peter Hoskins)

originally built in the twelfth century, is in Place Henri Deutsch de Meurthe (GPS 48.949814, 1.922657).

Poissy
Point 13: There has been a bridge over the Seine at Poissy since the time of Charlemagne. By the thirteenth century the bridge was in stone. The river was much wider in the fourteenth century and the bridge had thirty-seven arches; an idea of the width of the river in former times can be gained by looking at the distance covered by the remaining seven spans. In the fourteenth century there was a mill in the centre of the bridge, built in 1230 on the orders of Queen Blanche of Castile, wife of Louis VIII. The bridge was much modified over the centuries, with the addition of fortifications in the seventeenth century, and survived until destroyed by allied bombing in 1944. The remains of the old bridge are near the Rue de la Gare (GPS 48.933185, 2.037928).

Poissy was an important town for the Capetian dynasty, and the future King Louis IX was baptised in the twelfth-century collegiate church of Notre Dame, in Rue de l'Église (GPS 48.929653, 2.038016), in 1214.

The fourteenth-century gates of the Dominican priory, founded in 1304, survive in Rue de la Tournelle (GPS 48.928491, 2.037929), and there are some vestiges of the walls of the priory close to the junction

The old bridge at Poissy. (Peter Hoskins)

The fourteenth-century gates of the Dominican priory in Poissy. (Peter Hoskins)

of Rue de la Tournelle, and the Avenues Blanche de Castille and des Ursulines (GPS 48.926544, 2.038405). Edward is said to have lodged in the priory during his stay in Poissy.

A very short stretch of the medieval city walls is near 5 Boulevard Louis Lemelle (GPS 48.927122, 2.045000). The castle is said to have been burnt down by the Black Prince before his division moved on to St-Germain-en-Laye. It was so badly damaged that the ruins were demolished on the orders of King Charles V in 1369.

The only remaining stretch of the medieval walls of Poissy. (Peter Hoskins)

Maps

Maps at 1:25,000 and 1:100,000 scales		
Published by the *Institut National de l'Information Géographique et Forestière (IGN)* www.ign.fr		
Cartes de Randonnée – 1:25,000		
2012OT Forêt de Bord-Louviers, Elbeuf, Les Andelys	2113O Vernon	2114E Aubergenville, Guerville
2013E Pacy-sur-Eure	2113ET Mantes-la-Jolie, Boucles de la Seine, PNR du Vexin Français	2214ET Versailles, Forêts de Marly et de St Germain (also Tour 4)
TOP 100 – 1:100,000		
TOP100117 Caen/Evreux (also Tour 2)	TOP100108 Paris/Rouen (also Tour 4)	

How to Get There and Back by Public Transport

The Paris airports are convenient for this tour and are well connected to the city centre for onward travel by rail to Elbeuf. Ferries run from Portsmouth to Caen-Ouistreham and Le Havre. Railway services for this tour are provided by *SNCF* Basse-Normandie, Haute-Normandie and the Île-de-France Regions. Caen and Le Havre have main-line railway stations. There is a bus service between the port of Ouistreham and Caen (www.twisto.fr) but this does not operate during the evenings. There are buses from the ferry port in Le Havre to the railway station but this is only a few minutes' walk away. There is a train service from Caen to Elbeuf (Région Basse-Normandie) and Le Havre to Elbeuf via Rouen (Région Haute-Normandie). Elbeuf is accessible from Paris via Oissel. Regional trains from the Haute-Normandie Region provide a service to Pont-de-l'Arche, Louviers (bus), Gaillon-

Aubevoye (2km north of Gaillon), and Vernon-Giverny. The Île-de-France Region, also known as the Transilien, has an extensive network beyond Vernon, including Bonnières, Mantes-la-Jolie and Poissy. Timetables and route maps can be found on www.transilien.com. Tickets cannot be reserved for trains and buses on Transilien services.

Where to Stay and Where to Eat
The valley of the Seine is relatively densely populated and places to find refreshments are more plentiful than on other parts of the itinerary. Refreshments can be found at: Elbeuf, Pont-de-l'Arche, Criquebeuf-sur-Seine, Léry, Le Vaudreuil, Louviers, Gaillon, St-Pierre-d'Autils, Vernon, Épône, Ecquevilly and Poissy.

The local websites below give information on accommodation and refreshments for this tour:

www.pontdelarche.fr
www.ville-gaillon.fr
www.vernon27.fr
www.poissy-tourisme.fr
www.normandie-tourisme.fr

Tour Four
Poissy to Abbeville

This tour covers the route from Edward III's departure from Poissy on 16 August 1346, having crossed the Seine, until his crossing of the Somme at Blanchetaque on 24 August. The tour, of approximately 160km, starts in Poissy and finishes in Abbeville.

What Happened
The March to Blanchetaque
Philip had moved his army south through Paris on 15 August to prepare for the eventuality that Edward might respond to his challenge, sent on 14 August, to join in battle between 17 and 22 August. It is impossible to say whether or not Edward would have acted differently if he had received the challenge while still at Poissy (Point 1), but in the event he did not receive it until 17 August when he was at Auteuil, more than 50km north of Poissy.

So Edward continued his march northwards on 16 August to make for the intended rendezvous with the reinforcements due to arrive at Le Crotoy, leaving Poissy burning behind him and having destroyed the bridge. On the same day Philip moved to the village of Antony 10km south of Paris and 30km south-east of Poissy. If Philip wanted to pursue Edward, he would need to pass through Paris once again.

By the night of 16 August Edward's forces had moved 26km to Grisy-les-Plâtres (Point 2). The route initially took them across low-lying land between the rivers Seine and Oise, and then up onto higher ground. The next day, Thursday, 17 August, they moved on a further 25km over undulating terrain to Auteuil, only 11 km south-west of the important town of Beauvais (Point 3). While at Auteuil Edward replied to Philip's challenge, saying that if the French king had really wanted battle, then he could have come to him while he was at Poissy. He said that he would not be dictated to by Philip and that he would continue his march to bring comfort to his friends and punish those who

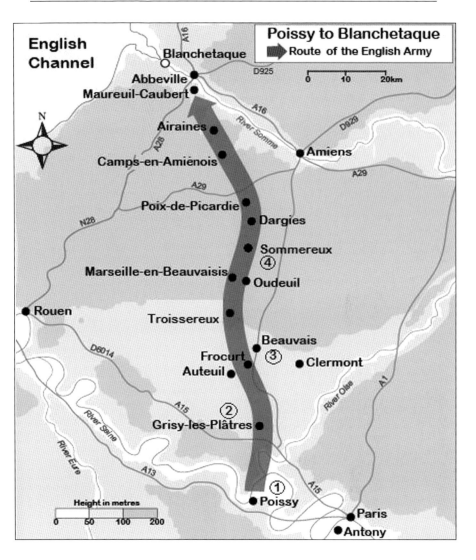

rebelled against his authority. Philip could have battle wherever he found him.

Edward was moving towards the Somme, but he was going to need to cross the river somewhere if he were to join up with Hastings and his Flemish army and meet the reinforcements and supplies en route to Le Crotoy. He knew the importance of speed and crossing the Somme before Philip could bring sufficient troops to bear to stop him.

He abandoned some of his baggage train and used captured horses to mount his infantry. Keeping his army focused on speed rather than plunder was no easy matter, with men in the division of his son the Black Prince being among the offenders. Valuable time was wasted attacking the village of Vessencourt, now absorbed within the commune of Frocourt, 7km south of Beauvais. The men were stopped from assaulting Beauvais itself, strongly defended with walls that had been repaired that year, but not before they had wasted further valuable time setting fire to suburbs, churches outside the walls, and adjoining villages and farms.

Philip responded quickly and decisively to the departure of the English from Poissy. He recrossed Paris and set off on a series of forced marches covering 40km a day to reach the Somme and cut off Edward. With Philip racing for the Somme, the French made life as difficult as they could for Edward by removing supplies from the countryside, forcing his men to forage far and wide and, as a consequence, inevitably slowing his progress. As Philip started to overhaul the English army near Beauvais the local population seem to have taken encouragement, gathering in armed bands to harry English troops detached from the main divisions.

After the time wasted near Beauvais the army moved less than 20km on Friday, 18 August as it made its way to Troissereux. On the Saturday the pace was better once more with 25km covered to Sommereux (Point 4), despite time taken out once again to burn another abbey, this time the Cistercian foundation at Beaupré near Marseille-en-Beauvaisis, and the villages of Oudeuil and Marseille-en-Beauvaisis. A similar distance was covered again on Sunday, 20 August to Camps-en-Amiénois (Point 5), passing via Poix-de-Picardie. This stage of the march was across more steeply undulating terrain than hitherto, and with the minor river Évoissons running in a narrow steep-sided valley, which would have slowed the progress of the wagon train.

Shortly after leaving Sommereux the English came across the castle at Dargies. It seems to have been unoccupied and it was looted and burned without opposition. The castle was never rebuilt and there is no trace of it today. Poix-de-Picardie was another matter entirely, walled and with a castle within the town and with the inhabitants, although their lord had left to join Philip's gathering army, manning the

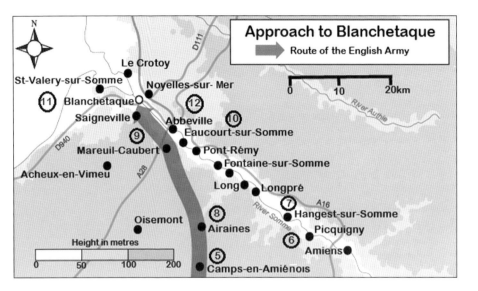

ramparts. With the French army close at hand, Edward's priority was to continue to the Somme, and he attempted to prevent an attack on the town. However, contrary to the express orders of the king, with sergeants twice being sent to order a cessation of the attack, and despite the example set of twenty men being hanged near Beauvais for burning the Benedictine abbey of St Lucien in defiance of the king's orders, the English soldiery could not resist the potential of rich pickings. The town and the castle were taken and Poix was burned. Somehow, despite these diversions, good progress was made, with 25km covered. However, such assaults inevitably took time, and this had its cost with Philip making up for being caught the wrong side of Paris when Edward left Poissy. When Edward was at Troissereux on 18 August, Philip was only 30km to his south-east at Clermont. Philip now drew ahead and by the time the English were at Camps-en-Amiénois, about 20km south of the Somme, the French had already reached the river. Philip himself was at Amiens on 20 August, in the company of Jean de Luxembourg, King of Bohemia, and the contingent he had brought from Paris. The balance of numbers was also now moving inexorably in Philip's favour. Edward was losing stragglers as he moved north, while Philip could count on adding to his army troops mustered at Amiens as well as those of the Count of Flanders which had been ordered to Abbeville.

Edward moved on just 10km on 21 August to Airaines (Point 8). The town was fortified, unusually with two castles within the walls. The first of these, built in the twelfth century and variously known as the chateau de l'Abbaye, because of its proximity to the priory and the church, and the chateau des Comtes de Ponthieu, and the second the chateau des Sires d'Airaines built in the following century. There is no record of the town either having been taken by assault or, despite the extensive defences, having put up a fight, and it seems that it had been evacuated before the arrival of the English. Elsewhere, however, there were signs of stiffening resistance, and on the approach to Airaines a force was threatening to attack the English rear-guard. Hugh Despenser and the Earl of Suffolk were sent to drive them off. Somewhat ill-advisedly, the French chose to fight rather than withdraw. Sixty men-at-arms were captured and more than 200 French killed.

Edward stayed at Airaines throughout the next day and night while scouting parties investigated the possibilities for crossing the Somme. The French had broken most of the bridges, and those that remained were strongly defended. Those in Abbeville and Amiens were defended by the town walls. In addition, the French were guarding every potential fording place between Amiens and the sea. Moreover, there was a series of castles on both sides of the river between Amiens and Abbeville, such as at Mareuil-Caubert (Point 9) on the left bank and Eaucourt-sur-Somme (Point 10) on the right, of which some ruins remain. On Tuesday, 22 August Warwick and Harcourt tried unsuccessfully to find a crossing of the river. An attempt to force a crossing was made at Pont-Rémy, where Warwick suffered losses to a force of mounted men-at-arms, archers and local levies commanded by John, King of Bohemia.

Warwick moved south-east from Pont-Rémy, up the valley of the Somme, passing through and burning the unfortified town of Fontaine-sur-Somme. About 3km beyond Fontaine-sur-Somme was a causeway leading to Long. The causeway was heavily defended and the bridge broken, and no attempt to cross was made. The next potential crossing was at Longpré, but this was also well defended and the ground difficult. Once again, no attempt was made to cross. The town was burned and Warwick moved on to Hangest-sur-Somme (Point 7). The bridge had been broken and the French were present in

The broad, flat valley of the Somme near Pont-Rémy, looking back towards the approach of the English towards the town. (Peter Hoskins)

force, and yet again a crossing could not be made. A final possibility would be at Picquigny (Point 6), a further 8km up-river. The town was surrounded by walls and towers and stood on cliffs above the Somme. It had four gates and had had a stone castle since 1066, which had been rebuilt in the fourteenth century and was contiguous with the town walls. Repairs had been carried out in 1346, and scouts reported that the town was well defended. Warwick turned away and returned to Airaines. Edward's position, if not desperate, was beginning to look serious. The shortage of supplies was becoming acute, with all stocks of bread exhausted and other supplies running low.

On the same day that Warwick was searching for a crossing of the Somme, although as yet unbeknown to him, events took a turn for the worse for Edward. Béthune had been besieged by Hugh Hastings and his Anglo-Flemish force since 14 August. The Flemings, who had become increasingly discouraged, not least because of a failed assault on 16 August and a successful sortie and raid on the siege camp by the garrison commander Godfrey d'Annequin on 22 August, abandoned

Looking east to the valley of the Somme from Monts de Caubert, south of Abbeville, where the bulk of the English army marched while elements searched for crossing points in the valley below. (Peter Hoskins)

the siege. They burnt their siege engines and headed for home. Edward had been in regular contact with Hugh Hastings but with the communications of the period only learned of the Flemish defection on either 24 or 25 August.

On Wednesday, 23 August, with the French apparently closing on his army, Edward had the choice of turning for battle or continuing to keep ahead of Philip. He chose the latter and set out from Airaines. He did so in some haste it seems, with one account claiming that when the French arrived later that day they ate food prepared and abandoned by the English. There were good reasons for his decision to continue to try to keep ahead of Philip rather than choose battle now. He already had a clear idea of his chosen site for the battle, he still hoped to join with Hastings and his Flemish troops and he still expected to receive his planned resupply and reinforcements at Le Crotoy before the battle which he planned to have at a time and place of his choosing. The army moved west initially towards the coast but at Oisemont turned north and lodged for the night at the village of Acheux-en-Vimeu. In contrast to Airaines, the local population at Oisemont gathered to resist the invader. They were no match for the English and were easily dispersed by a charge by mounted men-at-arms. Many were killed in the ensuing rout. More time was wasted in burning and pillaging the town before the army moved on to Acheux-en-Vimeu. During the day Edward had gone on to the high ground of Monts de Caubert, from where there was a clear view of Abbeville, 3km away, close to Mareuil-Caubert where the village and castle were destroyed and the church damaged. A sortie from Abbeville threatened the king's party, but the swift intervention of the Earl of Warwick drove the French back to Abbeville. It was clear that forcing a crossing by taking the bridge at Abbeville was not a practical proposition, and the king rejoined the army at Acheux-en-Vimeu.

Once he had reached the Somme, Philip had set about trapping Edward in a systematic way. He broke most of the bridges between Amiens and the sea, and secured potential crossing points with troops on the right bank of the river. From Amiens the French king then set out on the left bank, deploying his troops to trap the English between the river and the sea. As Edward moved on from Airaines, Philip moved into Abbeville, having deployed a strong force to defend the ford of Blanchetaque (Point 11). It must have seemed to Philip that he had Edward trapped and at his mercy. The result was quite the opposite.

At Acheux-en-Vimeu the English were 10km from the river. The need to find a crossing was now becoming critical. The only option was the ford of Blanchetaque between Abbeville and the sea. The two reasons most widely quoted to explain why the ford was called Blanchetaque, a corruption of the French for 'white stain', are that the name was either derived from the causeway being made of white chalk or because of a white chalk mark on the northern bank of the river used as a reference point to guide those crossing the river. We cannot be sure precisely where the ford was located. An eighteenth-century map shows the name Blanchetaque running down the centre of the river close to the estuary, which does not help locate the ford. The traditional view has been that the ford was somewhere near Saigneville, and there is a place marked on the 1:25,000 scale map called the *Chalet et Gué de Blanche Taque* (the chalet and ford of Blanche Taque) close by. The chalet, once a hunting lodge and now used as offices for management of the conservation of the Somme Bay wetlands, is a distinctive landmark. However, there are strong arguments in favour of the ford having been about 7km further downstream near the estuary crossing from St-Valery-sur-Somme to Le Crotoy.

The river has changed a great deal over the centuries, with construction of a canal and a railway and reclamation of land. In the fourteenth century the flood plain would have been inundated at high tide, and at low tide marshland covered in some places by shallow water. It is difficult today to visualize what Edward's army would have faced. However, from near the Chalet de Blanche Taque a good impression can be gained of the width of the flood plain of the Somme, a little over 3km wide between high ground on both sides rising 50m above sea level. Even today, with the water controlled by the modern works, the marshy nature of the area is evident and many of the tracks are built on low, elevated causeways. The medieval causeway is said to have been wide enough for twelve men abreast. It is possible that there was a central causeway constructed of chalk able to support wheeled vehicles with a wider area usable by horses and those on foot. Abbeville was a port in the Middle Ages, and the water level at high tide would have been sufficient to allow the passage of ships, so it would be vital to make the most of low tide.

According to some accounts Edward III was unaware of the ford and its existence was revealed by a Frenchman, Gobin Agace, from the nearby village of Mons-Boubert. It is said that he was a prisoner taken at Oisemont and that he revealed the location of the ford in exchange for his liberty and 100 gold *écus*. Others talk of an expatriate Yorkshireman giving information to the English. However, the County of Ponthieu had been in Edward's hands until ten years before, and some of the senior men in the English army knew the county. In particular, Bartholomew Burghersh had been seneschal of Ponthieu. It seems more likely than not that he knew of the ford. However, although the general location of the ford may have been known, it is possible that its precise nature was not. A squire in the service of the Flemish knight Wulfart Ghistels is said to have come to Edward at Acheux-en-Vimeu saying that he had found the crossing and that it

The wide flood plain of the Somme near the ford of Blanchetaque. (Peter Hoskins)

was practicable. When the army reached the ford, the squire is reported as having ridden up and down the river to demonstrate the width of the crossing. Whatever the truth of the matter, in the early hours of 24 August the English army set off for the river. When they arrived at Blanchetaque the strength of the French defenders was apparent. In addition they had to wait for the tide to fall further before a crossing could be attempted in the face of 500 French men-at-arms and 3,000 infantry drawn up in three ranks under the command of Godemar du Fay.

At about 8.00 a.m. 100 men-at-arms and 100 archers waded into the river with the objective of establishing a beach-head. Under the command of the Earl of Northampton and Reginald Cobham, the archers let loose when within range and the small English force drove the defenders back. As more English troops poured across, the beach-head expanded until finally du Fay's men broke and started to flee towards Abbeville. The English had crossed the Somme and escaped Philip's trap.

The Route by Car

Leave Poissy (Point 1) on the D190 and in Carrières-sous-Poissy turn right and follow the D22 through Grisy-les-Plâtres (Point 2) and then the D5 through Hénonville. Stay on the D5 until the junction with the D927, about 4km beyond St-Crépin-Ibouvillers. Follow the D927, D1001 and D139 into Beauvais (Point 3). Leave Beauvais on the D901 and follow this road through Troissereux and St-Omer-en-Chaussée, turning right onto the D72 1km after leaving St-Omer-en-Chaussée. Stay on the D72 until reaching the junction with the D56, about 4km beyond Prévillers. Follow the D56 through Sommereux (Point 4) and turn right onto the D108 1.5km after leaving Sommereux. On approaching Dargies turn left to follow an unnumbered road to join the D94c and then the D94 through Guizancourt. Shortly after passing a former mill on leaving the village, fork left onto and follow an unnumbered road to Poix-de-Picardie. Take the D901 from Poix-de-Picardie to Airaines via Camps-en-Amiénois (Point 5). To visit Picquigny (Point 6) and Hangest-sur-Somme (Point 7), take the D211 and D141 from Camps-en-Amiénois to Picquigny and then the D3 to Hangest-sur-Somme. Return to the main route at Airaines (Point 8) by taking the D69 to Soues and then the D936. Continue from Airaines on the D901 to Liercourt and turn left to follow the D3 through Mareuil-Caubert (Point 9). To visit the ruined castle of Eaucourt (Point 10) remain on the D901 through Liercourt and Pont-Rémy towards Abbeville. Turn left onto the Rue du Pont in Eaucourt-sur-Somme. The ruins are on the left close to the river. Retrace the route to Liercourt to return to the main route. In Mareuil-Caubert turn left onto the Rue de Villers and follow this unnumbered road to Moyenneville. Take the D22 to Toeufles and then follow an unnumbered road to Acheux-en-Vimeu. Join the D80 and at the junction with the D925 turn right towards Abbeville. At Miannay take the D86 to Cahon. Then follow minor, unnumbered roads, initially the Chemin du Long Rideau to Gouy and then the Chemin du Canal, cross the canal to Petit Port and continue to the intersection with the D40. Turn left and continue to Port-le-Grand. In the village, turn left by the railway halt (the road to the right is Rue Pascal), cross the railway and turn right to continue on the Chemin de Valois. Take the third turning to the left after about 2km. The turning is signposted Station Biologique de Blanchetaque (Point 11) et Ferme des Bouchers. To complete the tour, return to Petit Port and take the D40 to Abbeville (Point 12).

The Route on Foot and by Bike

Once away from the built-up and densely populated area around Poissy and Cergy-Pontoise this tour is largely across open, sparsely populated countryside. Most of the walking is along tracks and minor roads. The terrain is initially undulating, with the occasional valley to cross, but for the latter part is across the flat lands of northern Picardy.

Leave Poissy (Point 1) on the D190 and in Carrières-sous-Poissy turn right to follow the D22 through Chanteloup-les-Vignes, Courdimanche and Boissy-l'Aillerie to Grisy-les-Plâtres (Point 2). In Grisy-les-Plâtres take the Rue du Général de Gaulle and continue straight ahead on a track to rejoin the D22 800m north of the village.

> The track which is the continuation of the Rue du Général de Gaulle has a natural surface of packed earth and stone. It is in good condition, but an alternative route for the cyclist is to remain on the D22.

Continue on the D22 to Hénonville and then follow the D105 to Ivry-le-Temple. Turn right and follow the D619 through Haillancourt to the junction with the D923. Continue straight across the road and follow a track and then an unnumbered road across the D129 to the farm at Pontavesne. Beyond the farm follow a track once again to Valdampierre.

> The track from the D619/D923 junction as far as the woods near Montoisel has a natural surface of flint and earth. The road is then paved as far as Pontavesne, but the track beyond to Valdampierre once again has a stone and earth surface. An alternative route for the cyclist is to take the D923 from the junction with the D619 and then the D562 from Bléquencourt to Valdampierre.

Leave Valdampierre on the Rue du Général Leclerc and continue on this unnumbered road to Auteuil. Turn left onto the D2 in the village and then right onto an unnumbered road. Almost immediately after the road turns right through ninety degrees, take a path to the left. Follow this path to the D927. Stay on the D927 for 1.5km and then turn left on an unnumbered road through Vessencourt and rejoin the D927. The 1:25,000 map shows a number of paths through the Bois d'Auteuil and Bois de l'Équipée which seem to offer the prospect of staying clear of the D927 as far as Vessencourt. These paths no longer exist. After 800m on the D927 turn left onto the *GR126* footpath (which is poorly marked) and continue to the junction with the D93. Follow this road to the junction with the Avenue Jean Rostand, and then continue straight on along the Rue de Pontoise and D139 into Beauvais (Point 3).

The path north of Auteuil to the D927 and the section of the *GR126* both have stone and earth surfaces. A short section of track before the D93 through Les Grandes Vignes near Bongenoult is steep and the surface is poor. An alternative route for the cyclist beyond Auteuil is to turn right onto the D2 in the village and then left onto the D927. Shortly after this road crosses over the N13 there is an unnumbered road to the left which can be followed through Bongenoult to join the D93 and the main route into Beauvais.

Leave Beauvais on the Rue de la Mie au Roy. Just beyond the Base de Loisirs at the northern end of the lake Plan d'Eau du Canada, turn left onto a track and continue until reaching the railway. Turn right and follow the track parallel to the railway. On reaching the D616 turn right and follow the road to Troissereux. Go straight across the D901 and follow the Rue de Guehengnies to Guehengnies.

The initial stretch of track from the Rue de la Mie au Roy to the railway track has a chipped stone surface. The track parallel to the railway is a paved cycle path. To avoid the stone track stay on the Rue de la Mie au Roy and join the D901 to Troissereux.

In Guehengnies follow the unnumbered road through the village, turning left onto the Rue du Paradis Guehengnies, and then follow a track to Juvignies. Leave the village on the Rue du Quevremont. Turn left onto the D149 and then right onto the D11 through Luchy to the junction with the D9. Turn left and follow the D9 to the D149. Follow this road to Crèvecoeur-le-Grand.

The track between Guehengnies and Juvignies has a surface of packed earth and stone. An alternative route for cyclists is to stay on the unnumbered road through Guehengnies and continue towards Verderel-lès-Sauqueuse. Turn left to follow the D149 and then the D11 to rejoin the main route to Luchy.

Leave Crèvecoeur-le-Grand on the D151. At a roadside cross just beyond Hétomesnil turn right and follow an unnumbered road through Rieux. From Rieux take the Chemin de la Messé and follow this track to Sommereux.

The Chemin de la Messé is paved for 200m and then becomes a grass and earth surfaced track until 200m before joining the D124 near Sommereux. An alternative route for the cyclist is along the D151 and D56 from Hétomesnil to Sommereux via Le Hamel.

Leave Sommereux on the D56 and after 1.5km turn right onto the D108 to Dargies. From Dargies take a track north to join an unnumbered road to Lahaye-St-Romain.

The track north from Dargies is steep and has a poor surface of flint and earth. The alternative route for cyclists is to follow an unnumbered road which skirts round to the west of the village.

From Lahaye-St-Romain follow the D94 and D94c to Guizancourt. Leave the village on the D94. About 200m after crossing the river take the next left and follow an unnumbered road to Poix-de-Picardie. Leave Poix-de-Picardie on the D189. In Éplessier turn right and follow an unnumbered road to Thieulloy-l'Abbaye. Continue north on unnumbered roads and cross the D901 to follow a track to Gouy-l'Hôpital and then an unnumbered road to join the D901 near Lincheux-Hallivillers.

The track from the D901 to Gouy-l'Hôpital has a stone and earth surface. This track can be avoided by cyclists by taking the D901.

Follow the D901 to Camps-en-Amiénois. Turn right onto the D211 and take the first left onto an unnumbered road. Follow this north and join the *GR125* just north of the village by a roadside cross. About 2km north of Camps-en-Amiénois, at a junction with another unnumbered road, near the woods named the Bois de Vandricourt, continue straight ahead on a track which leads to the woods of the Bois de Warlus. There are several paths through the woods and care is needed to find the correct path to join the Chemin des Vaches. A small pavilion to the left of the path is a useful landmark. Cross the D901 and follow an unnumbered road to Warlus.

The track from the vicinity of the Bois de Vandricourt and through the Bois de Warlus is earth and stone and badly rutted in places. The Chemin des Vaches has a chalk and flint surface. The cyclist can avoid these tracks by turning left onto an unnumbered road near the Bois de Vandricourt and right onto the D901, rejoining the route above at the junction with the Chemin des Vaches.

In Warlus turn right onto the D18 and then left onto the D901. In Tailly turn left opposite a small monument and follow an unnumbered road and then a track to Laleu. On leaving Laleu take an unnumbered road and then a track past Le Mermont Farm to join a further unnumbered road and then follow the D96 into Airaines (Point 8).

The tracks from north-west of Tailly to Laleu and past Le Mermont Farm have earth and stone surfaces. An alternative for cyclists is to stay on the D901 beyond Tailly, turning left onto the D596 through Laleu and Métigny. Take the D96c and D96 to Airaines.

From Airaines take an unnumbered road and then a track north-west towards Hallencourt. Then take the D173 to the junction with the D928. Follow an unnumbered road through Béhen and Toeufles to Acheux-en-Vimeu.

The track beyond Dreuil to Hallencourt has a natural earth and stone surface. An alternative route for cyclists is to leave Airaines on the D938 and then follow the D173 through Allery to Hallencourt.

Take the D80 from Acheux-en-Vimeu through Franleu and 1km north of the village follow an unnumbered road to join the D106 into Boubert. Now follow the D403 to Boismont. Turn left onto the D3 and, after about 200m, turn right onto an unnumbered road. After 1km the road turns sharply right to cross the canal from Abbeville to St-Valery. Continue on this road until the junction with a road which runs parallel to the railway embankment, turn right onto this road and continue for 1.5km. A short distance down the road on the right, the Chemin de Blanchetaque, is the Chalet de Blanchetaque (Point 11). From Blanchetaque return to the road parallel to the railway and continue to Port-le-Grand. Follow the D40 and turn right onto the

D86. Cross the canal and turn left to follow the towpath on the southern bank into Abbeville (Point 12).

N.B. The map shows a number of paths in the stretch of flood plain between Boismont and Port-le-Grand which seem to offer a shorter route than the one described above. Some of these are impracticable and others are private and not accessible. Attempting to follow them is likely to result in a longer walk than planned!

What to See
Poissy
Point 1: *See* Tour Three, pages 123–5.

Grisy-les-Plâtres
Point 2: The church of St Caprais in the Place de l'Église (GPS 49.131154, 2.050422) was built in the thirteenth century and restored in the sixteenth century.

Beauvais
Point 3: Beauvais has a particularly rich heritage of buildings surviving from the Middle Ages. Inside the area once protected by the town walls

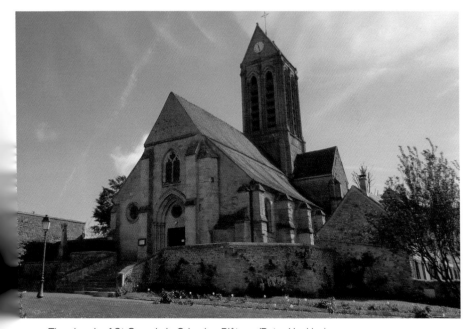

The church of St Caprais in Grisy-les-Plâtres. (Peter Hoskins)

are the magnificent thirteenth-century cathedral of St Pierre, with the adjoining vestiges of the earlier eleventh-century cathedral of Notre-Dame de la Basse-Oeuvre, in Rue St Pierre (GPS 49.432296, 2.081177), the remains of the collegiate church of St Barthélemy in Place St Barthélemy (GPS 49.431556, 2.082128) and the bishop's palace in Rue de Musée (GPS 49.432624, 2.080400) which now houses the Musée Départementale de l'Oise (www.mudo.oise.fr). Also within the old city is the twelfth- and thirteenth-century church of St Étienne in the Rue de l'Étamine (GPS 49.428678, 2.080079) and some restored fourteenth-century houses at 4–6 Rue de l'École-de-Chant (GPS 49.432001, 2.078994) and 1 Rue du Tourne-Broche (GPS 49.432089, 2.078562). The town was well fortified in the Middle Ages with the line of the walls following closely the modern inner boulevard defined to the north by the Boulevard Dr Lamotte, Boulevard du Général de Gaulle to the east, Boulevard A Briand to the south and the Boulevard Loisel to the west.

The fourteenth-century gatehouse of the bishop's palace in Beauvais. (Peter Hoskins)

The twelfth-century church of St Étienne in Beauvais. (Peter Hoskins)

A stretch of the town walls in Beauvais adjoining the Tour Boileau. (Peter Hoskins)

The fourteenth-century main gate to the close of the abbey of St Lucien. (Peter Hoskins)

The chapel and residential buildings of the leper house of St Lazare. (Peter Hoskins)

There are vestiges of the walls and the tower Tour Boileau in the south-west of the town near the Boulevard St-Jean (GPS 49.426442, 2.075185), although construction of the tower did not begin until 1376. Outside the perimeter of the defended town was the lepers' house of St Lazare. There are extensive remains at 203 Rue de Paris (GPS 49.414605, 2.101285) with its twelfth-century church, and residential quarters and grange dating from the thirteenth century. It is open from 11.00 to 18.00 from Tuesday to Sunday between 1 April and 30 September. Also outside the walls was the abbey of St Lucien, burnt contrary to the king's orders. The church and elements of the external walls remain in Rue St-Lucien and Rue Louis Prache (GPS 49.442498, 2.079178).

Sommereux
Point 4: The thirteenth- and fourteenth-century church of St Aubin in Rue Chantal Garzuel (GPS 49.680641, 1.992136) was formerly a Templar chapel.

Camps-en-Amiénois
Point 5: The church of St Nicholas in Rue de Séhu (GPS 49.880566, 1.971555) has elements remaining from the thirteenth century.

Picquigny
Point 6: Picquigny was a well defended town on the Somme. There are

The church of St Aubin in Sommereux. (Peter Hoskins)

The church of St Nicholas in Camps-en-Amiénois. (Peter Hoskins)

Construction of the church of St Martin in Picquigny started in 1066. (Peter Hoskins)

The fourteenth-century barbican of Picquigny castle. (Peter Hoskins)

substantial remains of the castle in the town (GPS 49.942904, 2.142302). The interiors of the buildings are not open to visitors, but the grounds and exterior are, nevertheless, worth seeing. The twelfth- and thirteenth-century collegiate church of St Martin (GPS 49.943166, 2.142173), built to replace an earlier castle chapel, is within the curtilage of the castle.

Hangest-sur-Somme

Point 7: Scouts looking for a crossing of the Somme passed via Hangest. The church of Ste Marguerite, Rue Jean Baptiste Carpentier, with its thirteenth-century bell-tower survives (GPS 49.979855, 2.06518).

The church of Ste Marguerite in Hangest-sur-Somme. (Peter Hoskins)

Airaines

Point 8: Edward III paused at Airaines while his scouts were looking for a crossing of the Somme in the valley below. The priory church of Notre-Dame in the Rue des Buttes (GPS 49.9625, 1.939444) was built around 1130. The adjoining priory was destroyed during the Burgundian occupation in 1422 and rebuilt in the sixteenth century. The original parish church of St Denis in Rue St Denis (GPS 49.965094, 1.945351) was also built in the twelfth century, but the current building dates from the sixteenth century. The chateau de l'Abbaye, or the chateau des Comtes de Ponthieu, stood on the hill approximately 150m to the north-west of the church of Notre-Dame.

The castle had been garrisoned by the Burgundians in 1422. It was razed by King Louis XI in 1472, and only the motte remains, which can be seen from the Rue du Chateau de Ponthieu (GPS 49.963051, 1.93856). The château des sires d'Airaines was destroyed in the sixteenth century and a new castle was built on the same site the following century. Two towers of the later castle, known as Les Tours de Luynes, survive in Rue de Luynes (GPS 49.965135,1.939826).

The church of Notre-Dame in Airaines. (Peter Hoskins)

Les Tours de Luynes on the site of the château des sires d'Airaines. (Peter Hoskins)

Mareuil-Caubert

Point 9: Part of the English army passed this way looking for a crossing of the Somme. The church of St Christophe on the D3 (GPS 50.068465, 1.830001) was built in the eleventh century. It was partially destroyed, along with the village and the castle, by Edward III's army. The façade, nave and some of the choir survived, and repairs and additions were made during the fourteenth and fifteenth centuries. The wooden porch in front of the north door dates from the sixteenth century. The castle of Mareuil-Caubert stood on the higher ground about 150m north-west of the church

The church of St Christophe in Mareuil-Caubert. (Peter Hoskins)

The remains of the castle at Eaucourt-sur-Somme. (Peter Hoskins)

Eaucourt-sur-Somme

Point 10: The castle at Eaucourt-sur-Somme, in the Rue du Pont close to the Somme, was one of a number of castles along the stretch of river between Abbeville and Amiens where English scouts searched for crossings. Along with other similar castles along the river it suffered at the hands of the Burgundians in 1421 (GPS 50.062077, 1.881364). However, some vestiges remain and a number of activities are organized here during the summer: www.chateau-eaucourt.com.

Blanchetaque

Point 11: The eastern end of the possible position of the old ford of Blanchetaque near Saigneville where the English crossed the Somme is marked by the Chalet de Blanche Taque (GPS 50.160103, 1.724893), formerly a hunting lodge and now used as administrative offices for management of the Somme estuary wetlands. The chalet has, of course, no historic significance but it serves as a useful reference point to gain an impression of the Somme valley near the ford.

Abbeville

Point 12: The town suffered a great deal in 1940. Much of the town is post-war and drab and uninteresting, but the thirteenth-century belfry in Rue Gontier Patin (GPS 50.107166, 1.832962) survives.

The Abbeville belfry. (Peter Hoskins)

Tour Five

Abbeville to Calais via Crécy-en-Ponthieu

This tour starts from Abbeville and covers the route from the crossing of the Somme by Edward III's army at Blanchetaque through the battlefield at Crécy-en-Ponthieu and then to Calais. It covers approximately 160km.

What Happened
The Advance to Crécy-en-Ponthieu
On Thursday, 24 August 1346 Edward III successfully completed his crossing of the Somme at the ford of Blanchetaque. A mixed force of men-at-arms and archers had crossed first and established a beach-head on the far bank, and had driven back a substantial defending force under the command of Godemar du Fay, thus allowing the army to cross.

The tidal nature of the river had required that the crossing was made quickly and efficiently, but once the English were across and the tide rose again the opportunities for pursuit by the French were limited. Philip had left Abbeville (Point 1) that day with the aim of catching the English between the Somme and the sea. By the time he arrived near Blanchetaque (Point 2) late in the day Edward had already crossed and the tide had come in, precluding any thoughts of pursuit for the time being. The way was now clear for Edward to move north at will.

After the English crossed the Somme, the French guarding the ford fled, some heading for Abbeville and others rallying in the village of Sailly-Bray 5km north of Blanchetaque. The Earl of Warwick's men pursued and cut down those fleeing to Abbeville. French losses at Blanchetaque and in the immediate aftermath are said to have been around 2,000. However, despite the success of the crossing Edward's

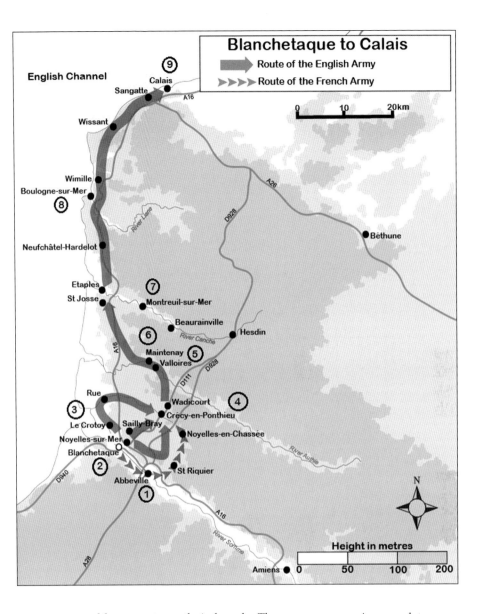

men could not rest on their laurels. There was a pressing need to replenish supplies.

Hugh Despenser was therefore despatched on a foraging raid. In the afternoon after the crossing of the river Noyelles-sur-Mer was sacked and Le Crotoy (Point 3) was burned in the evening, despite resistance from the Genoese garrison. A further raiding party in search of supplies took and burned Rue 10km north of Noyelles. Cattle and provisions were taken from Le Crotoy, along with wine aboard ships in the harbour, but there was no sign of the English reinforcements and supplies which should have arrived off-shore at Le Crotoy on 20 August. Indeed, the ships had still not been loaded and the men had not yet been assembled. With the failure to despatch reinforcements and the defection of the Flemings, Edward would now have to make do with his original army, depleted somewhat by casualties and the small force he had left at Caen.

Meanwhile the two armies faced each other across the river for the rest of the day and continued to watch each other for most of the next. Some diversion was provided by a challenge issued by a French knight, who wished to prove his love for a lady, for the English to send a knight to joust with him three times. Thomas Colville came forward to meet the challenge and the jousts started. After the second joust a shield was broken and the two men decided that to continue would be too dangerous. They are said to have become firm friends.

With Edward's men waiting in strength on the opposite banks of the Somme the risk of defeat would have been high if Philip had attempted to force a crossing, and the following morning, Friday, 25 August, Philip and his army disengaged and returned to Abbeville. Edward could now move off safely, and the army headed towards Crécy-en-Ponthieu (Point 4). The army was organized in three battles, or divisions, and it appears that they moved independently. The main body marched directly through the forest along an axis close to the modern D111. One division took a more northerly route via Le Crotoy, firing the town in passing, and Rue, while the other swept round to the south via St-Riquier. The army reassembled for the night on the eastern edge of the forest. The next day it moved about 4km to take up position near the village of Crécy-en-Ponthieu. The conventional view has long been that Edward, having concluded that he could not outrun the French army, elected to stand and fight. However, an alternative view is that he had all along intended to fight Philip if the circumstances were right. Whatever the truth of the matter, Crécy had two advantages: it was home ground in a sense since the County of Ponthieu had been in English hands between 1279 and 1330, and in addition the ridge running north-east from Crécy towards Wadicourt provided a strong position to draw up the English army.

On returning to Abbeville Philip found that the bridges had been badly damaged by the earlier crossing of the army and hasty repairs were needed to cope with the returning troops and wagons. It was not until the next day, Saturday, 26 August, that Philip moved off in pursuit of the English, taking the Hesdin road from Abbeville. The French followed a route to the east of the forest of Crécy, which at the time covered much of the land between the Somme and the Authie 20km to the north, passing by St-Riquier and Noyelles-en-Chaussée towards the road from Amiens to Montreuil-sur-Mer (Point 7). As Philip advanced beyond St-Riquier news reached him from scouts that Edward's army had passed through the forest of Crécy, crossed the Maye and was in the vicinity of the fortified village of Crécy-en-Ponthieu, about 15km to the north-west. Philip sent out further scouts, led by the Swiss knight Henri le Moine, to gather more precise intelligence on the English position. By the time they returned with the news that the English were drawn up in battle order between the villages of Crécy and Wadicourt, the leading elements of the French army, probably approaching along the road that has been named the

The Chemin de l'Armée to the south of Crécy, traditionally the road from Abbeville taken by the French army on the way to the battlefield. (Peter Hoskins)

Chemin de l'Armée, were barely 5km from Edward's men. The events that followed, resulting in the disastrous defeat for Philip, are described in Tour Six, the guide to the battlefield.

The March to Calais
After the battle Edward's army remained on the battlefield on Sunday, 27 August. The following morning French heralds arrived asking for a three-day truce, which was granted, to allow the dead to be collected from the battlefield and buried. That day the English moved off towards Calais, stopping for the next two nights near the Cistercian abbey of Valloires (Point 5) and the nearby village of Maintenay (Point 6) about 14km north of Crécy. The approach to Valloires from the battlefield took the army down into the valley of the Authie near Valloires.

On Wednesday, 30 August the march was resumed, with the army probably crossing the 1km flood plain of the Authie near Maintenay. There is a climb of 90m out of the river valley, but once on the higher ground the going would have been relatively easy across gently undulating terrain to St-Josse 15km further north-west. The army was moving once again on a broad front, burning and pillaging as it went.

On the Thursday the English moved on to Neufchâtel-Hardelot. The route took them across the river Canche, probably to the south-east of Étaples, and then up onto the high ground where the going was more difficult over steeply undulating terrain. They stayed in the vicinity of Neufchâtel-Hardelot. Just 4 km to the north-west was the thirteenth-century castle of Hardelot. The present building on the site was built in the nineteenth century. There is no record of the castle having been assaulted, and on Saturday, 2 September, having burned the town, the English moved on to Wimille, crossing the Liane and raiding Boulogne (Point 8) as they did so.

Edward stayed at Wimille for two nights. He was now only 30km from Calais (Point 9), and it seems that he took the opportunity of this pause to assess the situation with his advisers and decide on the next step. Despite the crushing victory at Crécy, it would have been evident that little of strategic value had been achieved since the landing at St-Vaast-la-Hougue almost eight weeks earlier. Towns and fortresses had been destroyed, but Edward did not have the means to occupy and control the territory through which he had passed. Calais was better placed and more defensible as a base for English expeditions to France than ports in Normandy and it was decided to capture Calais and the surrounding coastal area. On Monday, 4 September the army moved, initially across undulating terrain via Wissant before descending into the low-lying marshland near Sangatte. The scene was now set for the long siege of Calais which was to last until 3 August the following year. The town remained in English hands for more than two centuries before falling to the French in 1558.

En route between Crécy and Calais there had been widespread destruction and looting, but with some towns, such as Hesdin, Montreuil-sur-Mer and Boulogne, which had been well garrisoned and were fortified, faring better than others. There were unsuccessful attacks on Montreuil-sur-Mer and Boulogne resulting in the burning and looting of the suburbs, but no serious attempts were made to take these towns. Boulogne, however, was unfortunate in that later in September English ships returned and attacked the unprotected suburbs in the low town once again. Beaurainville, probably raided during the advance to St-Josse, and Étaples, although defended by a twelfth-century castle which resisted attack, were less fortunate and were stormed and sacked. Similarly, Wissant, 14km beyond Wimille was razed. The port of Wissant, however, seems to have remained in operation since on 29 October 1346 Queen Philippa landed here on the way to Sangatte to join Edward III engaged in the siege of Calais.

The approach to Wissant, a more important port in the Middle Ages than today. It was notable for the departure of Thomas Becket for England in 1170 before his assassination in Canterbury cathedral. (Peter Hoskins)

The Route by Car

This tour starts in Abbeville (Point 1) and rejoins the route of Edward III's army after visiting his crossing point of the Somme at Blanchetaque (Point 2). Leave Abbeville on the D40 to Port-le-Grand. In the village, turn left by the railway halt, cross the railway and turn right to continue on the Chemin de Valois. Take the third turning to the left after about 2km. The turning is signposted Station Biologique de Blanchetaque et Ferme des Bouchers. From Blanchetaque, retrace the route to the Chemin des Valois and on to Port-le-Grand. Turn left and follow the D40 and D140 to Noyelles-sur-Mer. To visit Le Crotoy (Point 3) leave Noyelles on the D140 and then take the D940 and D104. Return to Noyelles and then take the D111 through Sailly-Bray to Nouvion. Turn right onto the D1001 for about 400m and then left to follow the D111 again through the forest of Crécy to Crécy-en-Ponthieu (Point 4).

Leave Crécy initially on the D111 and then fork left to follow the D12 to Ligescourt. Now take the D212 to the junction with the D192 near Dominois. Turn left and follow the D192 through Valloires (Point 5). About 2km beyond the abbey at Valloires turn right onto an unnumbered road to Maintenay (Point 6). In the village turn left onto the D119. Just beyond Roussent turn right onto the D139E1 and after 1km turn left onto the D140. After passing through Le Puits-Bérault turn right onto the D901. In Wailly-Beaucamp turn left onto the D143E3. In Airon-St-Vaast turn right to take the D143E2. After 250m turn left into the Rue du Château. After 1km turn left onto the D143E1 and then almost immediately turn right onto the D144E2. Follow this road to St-Josse. To visit Montreuil-sur-Mer (Point 7) follow the D901 from Wailly-Beauchamp and then from Montreuil-sur-Mer take the D939 to Étaples.

From St-Josse take the D144 and then the D143 and the D940 into Étaples. Continue on the D940 through Neufchâtel-Hardelot to Boulogne-sur-Mer (Point 8). Take the D96 and then the D237E3 from Boulogne to Rupembert. Then follow the D237 through Wimille and Bazinghen to the junction with the D191 at Grand-Maison. Follow the D191 for 3km and turn left to follow the D238 to Wissant. Now follow the D940 to Calais (Point 9).

The Route on Foot and by Bike

The route crosses a variety of terrain, from the flat flood plain of the Somme across gently undulating terrain and then, beyond Étaples and the river Canche, more hilly countryside before descending into the low-lying land around Calais. Some of the route is through urban areas but most of it is through countryside on minor roads and tracks with a final stretch along a coast path.

Leave Abbeville (Point 1) on the towpath on the southern bank of the Canal Maritime d'Abbeville à St-Valery and continue to the D86. Turn right to follow this road through Petit-Port to the D40. Turn left and follow the road into Port-le-Grand. In the village turn left to cross the railway line on the crossing, and turn right to follow the Chemin des Valois. Follow this road to Noyelles-sur-Mer, passing the Chalet du Gué de Blanche Taque (Blanchetaque) (Point 2) on the left after 2km. N.B. Do not be tempted to stay on the towpath beyond the D86: the track on the map between the canal and the chalet past the Ferme des Bouchers is private and not open to the public.

From Noyelles-sur-Mer take the D111 through Sailly-Bray and Nouvion to Crécy-en-Ponthieu (Point 4). An alternative route through Crécy forest is to turn left onto a grass track 1.5km after entering the forest onto the Sentier de Nouvion à Marcheville. This track rejoins the D111 at the Hutte des Vieux Chênes.

The Sentier de Nouvion à Marcheville is grass-covered and potholed. It is muddy in wet weather. The alternative for the cyclist is to remain on the D111.

Continue on the D111 through Crécy and then fork left to follow the D12 to Ligescourt. Follow the D212 from Ligescourt for 3.5km until the road swings to the right. Continue straight ahead on an unnumbered road to join the D192 just short of Dominois. Take the D192 through Valloires (Point 5). At the Petit Préaux turn right and follow an unnumbered road across the river Authie to Maintenay (Point 6). Turn left onto the D119. The road turns north in Roussent. Just beyond the Auberge des Étangs take the D139E1 and then after 1km turn left to follow the D140 through Le Puits Bérault to the D901. Turn right onto this road and after 150m turn left to follow the D140 once again. Turn right onto a track 500m after passing a small oratory on a crossroads near Ébruyères. Stay on this track across the D142. Turn left at the junction with the D143E3.

The track from near Ébruyères is paved for a short distance and then has a natural stone and earth surface, which is potholed in places, to the junction with the D142. The track is paved for the next 500m, as far as Collen, but then has a stone and earth surface to the junction with the D143E3. An alternative route for cyclists is to take the D901 from the junction with the D140 near Le Puits Bérault and turn left onto the D143E3 in Wailly-Beauchamp to rejoin the main route.

In Airon-St-Vaast turn right onto the D144E2. After 250m turn left into the Rue du Château and follow this road to the E143E1. Turn left and then almost immediately right onto the D144E2. Stay on this road to St-Josse. Take the D144 and D143 through Villiers to Trépied. Some 200m beyond the junction with the D940 turn right and follow the Chemin de la Nouvelle Digue to rejoin the D940 and follow this road into Étaples.

Leave Étaples on the Avenue François Mitterand, which becomes the Rue d'Étaples. Turn left on an unnumbered road past Le Fayel near Lefaux and turn right onto the D148E5 and pass under the autoroute A16. Turn left 1.5km after the autoroute, just before reaching Widehem, onto an unnumbered road which subsequently becomes a track. The track crosses the A16 once again. Cross over the D308 onto an unnumbered road and after 800m turn left and follow the Rue de l'Église into Neufchâtel-Hardelot.

The road after leaving the D148E5 near Widehem becomes a track after 500m. It is paved in places but for most of the way the surface is stone and earth. Beyond the A16 it is badly potholed and susceptible to being muddy in wet weather. An alternative for the cyclist is to remain on the D148E5 and on leaving Widehem turn left onto the Rue de la Croix Norbert. Turn left on reaching the D113 and follow this road to the junction with the D215 at La Buqueuse on the outskirts of Neufchâtel-Hardelot. Turn left onto the Rue des Allées into the village.

Turn left off the Rue de l'Église in Neufchâtel-Hardelot into the Rue des Sautoirs, cross the D940, turn right into the Rue de la Basse Flaque, left into the Rue de la Rivière and then first right into the Rue du Hêtre.

Continue on this road which after about 800m becomes a forest path. Follow the path to the junction with the D119. Take this road through Condette to Écault.

> The forest path beyond Neufchâtel-Hardelot has a grass surface with deep potholes and can be muddy. An alternative for cyclists is to remain on the Rue de la Rivière and join the D119. Follow this road through Condette to Écault.

From Écault stay on the D119 towards Équihen-Plage. After 1.5km turn right along a track. After 700m this track becomes an unnumbered road. Follow the road to Outreau and then make your way to Boulogne-sur-Mer (Point 8).

> The track between the D119 and the unnumbered road which leads to Outreau has a grass surface. The unnumbered road is paved but the surface is in poor condition. As a local notice puts it, 'believe it or not this road has not been bombarded for seventy years'. An alternative route for cyclists is to stay on the D119 through Outreau to Boulogne-sur-Mer.

Leave Boulogne-sur-Mer on the Route du Chemin Vert which passes the Napoleonic Colonne de la Grande Armée. In La Poterie take the Route de la Poterie and then join and follow the D237 through Wimille to Slack. From Slack take an unnumbered road, the Rue du Pré Communal, to Raventhum. Continue on the Rue de Ferquent, initially a paved road but which after 1.5km becomes a track for the remainder of the distance to Onglevert. Turn left onto the D191 for 150m. Turn right and follow an unnumbered road through Warincthun. This road becomes the D249 near Ausques. At a Y junction 500m beyond Ausques, fork left onto the Rue d'Inghen and after 200m turn right and follow a track for 800m. On reaching the D238 turn left and follow this road into Wissant.

> The unpaved section of the track to Onglevert has a stone and earth surface. It is in reasonable condition but with some potholes. The track between the Rue d'Inghen and D238 has a rutted grass and earth surface. An alternative route for cyclists is to turn right onto the

D119E1 in Raventhum. Continue on this road and the D237 to Grand Maison. Follow unnumbered roads north through Ricques-Maninghen. Join the D249 near Ausques and follow this road to the D238. Turn left and follow this road into Wissant.

In Wissant join the coast path, *GR120*, which is initially along the beach. When the tide is out the walker can remain on the beach as far as Cran d'Escalles, where steps lead from the beach to higher ground and the path can be rejoined climbing up onto Cap Blanc Nez. However, great caution is required since the tide can come in rapidly up the gently shelving beach. The beach is bordered by sand dunes as far as St-Pô but beyond there are steep, high cliffs and the walker risks being trapped beneath the cliffs. Until St-Pô, about 2km before the Cran d'Escalles, it is possible to leave the beach using wooden steps. The last opportunity is near St-Pô where there are some houses and an unnumbered road comes close to the beach (GPS 50.905815, 1.682857). The *GR120* can be followed to Calais (Point 9), but in Sangatte a section of the path which originally ran along the dyke has been closed for safety reasons following the collapse of part of the dyke. The *GR120* now follows the D940 for 2km but the original path can be rejoined near Ferme Baey.

The *GR120* between Wissant and Calais runs along the beach in places, but for some sections the path is along grass paths above the cliffs between St-Pô and Sangatte and on paths through scrubland behind the sand dunes between Sangatte and Calais. The alternative cycle route is to follow the D940 from Wissant to Calais.

What to See
Abbeville
Point 1: *See* Tour Four, page 153.

Blanchetaque
Point 2: *See* Tour Four, page 152.

Le Crotoy
Point 3: The church of St Pierre, with its thirteenth-century tower, is in Rue de l'Église (GPS 50.214834, 1.624704). There are remains of the

first castle, built in 1150, in Rue du Château (GPS 50.214834, 1.624704).

Crécy-en-Ponthieu
Point 4: *See* Tour Six, pages 192–6.

Valloires
Point 5: The abbey of Valloires, on the D192 (GPS 50.349092, 1.819987), was founded in the twelfth century, but damage caused during the Wars of Religion and a series of disasters in the seventeenth century resulted in the abbey being substantially rebuilt later that century. It is claimed locally that Jean de Luxembourg, the blind King of Bohemia, died in the abbey of his wounds sustained at the battle of Crécy. Guided visits are provided and some of the abbey has been turned over to use as a hotel (www.abbaye-valloires.com).

Maintenay
Point 6: The church of St Nicholas, in Rue de l'Église (GPS 50.366278, 1.810166), has been much modified over the centuries but elements date from the original thirteenth-century church.

The church of St Nicholas in Maintenay. (Peter Hoskins)

Montreuil-sur-Mer
Point 7: Montreuil-sur-Mer, headquarters for the British army in the First World War, was well defended in the fourteenth century and it is little surprise that it escaped relatively unscathed as the English army moved north after the battle. The walls have been added to and modified over the centuries, but elements of the ramparts and towers dating from the thirteenth century can still be seen to the west of the town. The twelfth-century abbey church of St Saulve is in Place Gambetta (GPS 50.464016, 1.762877).

Boulogne-sur-Mer
Point 8: Boulogne has a rich heritage from the Middle Ages. The town walls, built between 1227 and 1231, survive, with seventeen towers linking four gates in Rue d'Aumont, the Porte Gayole (GPS 50.723561, 1.614962), Rue du Puits d'Amour, the Porte de Degrès (GPS 50.723827, 1.612250), the Place de la Résistance, Porte des Dunes (GPS 50.725216, 1.612158), and the Porte Neuve in Rue de Lille (GPS 50.726465, 1.616094). The twelfth-century belfry in the Place de la Résistance (GPS 50.724914, 1.612837) was originally a fortification in its own right. Completing the surviving fortifications is the castle, accessed from Rue de Bernet (GPS 50.725540, 1.616321), construction of which started in 1231. Much of the castle dates from the thirteenth century with some earlier Roman vestiges and later sixteenth-century additions. The castle houses a museum which is open in the mornings and afternoons for most of the year (www.tourisme-boulognesurmer. com). Outside the walled town stands the church of St Nicolas in Place Dalton (GPS 50.723234, 1.606742); much of the church dates from the eighteenth century but the tower is thirteenth century.

Calais
Point 9: Calais suffered extensive damage in the Second World War. However, the thirteenth-century watch-tower, the Tour du Guet (GPS 50.958927, 1.849447), in the Place d'Armes and the church of Notre-Dame (GPS 50.958616, 1.853117) in Rue Notre Dame survive from the Middle Ages. The town had been taken in 1347 after a siege lasting almost a year. It remained an English possession, and a

The church of Notre Dame was started in the thirteenth century. Further work was carried out during the English occupation, when it was within the diocese of Canterbury. (Peter Hoskins)

The thirteenth-century watch-tower in Calais. (Peter Hoskins)

Rodin's sculpture of the burghers of Calais. (Peter Hoskins)

valuable but expensive to maintain bridgehead for English monarchs, until 1558.

In front of the Hôtel de Ville, just off the Boulevard Jacquard (GPS 50.952452, 1.853378), is a sculpture by Rodin commemorating the surrender of the town to Edward III by the burghers of Calais in 1347.

Maps

Maps at 1:25,000 and 1:100,000 scales
Published by the *Institut National de l'Information Géographique et Forestière (IGN)* www.ign.fr

Cartes de Randonnée – 1:25,000		
2207O Abbeville (also Tour 4)	2107OT Le Tréport (also Tour 4)	2106ET Le Crotoy, Fort-Mahon-Plage
2105ET Le Touquet-Paris-Plage, Berck	2104ET Boulogne-su-Mer	2103ET Calais

TOP 100 – 1:100,000	
TOP100103 Amiens/Arras (also Tour 4)	TOP100101 Lille/Boulogne-sur-Mer

How to Get There and Back by Public Transport
Beauvais, Lille and Paris airports are all practical for this tour. Abbeville, Étaples, Boulogne-sur-Mer and Calais are all served by main-line trains. Regional trains from Picardie and Nord-Pas de Calais serve stations between Calais and Abbeville including Neufchâtel-Hardelot-Plage and Wimille-Wimereux.

Where to Stay and Where to Eat
Refreshments can be found in Noyelles-sur-Mer, Crécy-en-Ponthieu, Ligescourt, Argoules, Maintenay, Roussent, St-Josse, Étaples, Neufchâtel-Hordelot, Condette, Boulogne, Wimille, Wissant, Escalles, Sangatte and Calais.

The local websites below give information on accommodation and refreshment for this tour:

www.abbeville-tourisme.com
www.crecyenponthieu.com
www.tourisme-montreuillois.com
www.hardelot-tourisme.com
www.etaples-tourisme.com
www.calais-guide.co.uk/tourist-office.html
www.tourisme-boulognesurmer.com

Tour Six

A Guide to the Battlefield

This tour describes what happened from the arrival of King Edward's army at Crécy-en-Ponthieu on Friday, 25 August 1346, the subsequent battle the following day, and events until the departure of the English towards Calais on Monday, 28 August.

What Happened
Where Did it Happen?

There are numerous sources for the battle of Crécy, some based on first-hand accounts, and these give a good overall picture of the course of the battle. However, they are tantalizingly short of detail and leave many uncertainties over the disposition and formations of the armies and the tactics employed. It is impossible to say with certainty precisely where the battle was fought. There is a very strong case, based on tradition, topography and toponymy, for the generally accepted location of the battlefield to the east of the village of Crécy-en-Ponthieu with the main fighting orientated along the Vallée des Clercs, said to have been where clerks from Crécy Grange, a dependency of the abbey of Valloires, counted the dead after the battle. Other toponyms associated with the battle are the Chemin de la Armée, along which, according to tradition, the French army approached Crécy, the Croix du Roi de Bohème, where the blind King of Bohemia is said to have died after the battle, and the Marché à Carognes where dead horses are traditionally believed to have been buried. All support the general location of the battlefield. The likely English position is marked by a viewing platform where a windmill, said to have been used by King Edward III to observe the battle, is believed to have stood, and by the name of a parcel of land, Le Guidon, just behind the platform. Further afield, 7km to the south-west of Crécy in Forest-L'Abbaye, is the church of the Nativité-de-la-Vierge, formerly a Templar chapel, where the English dead are said to

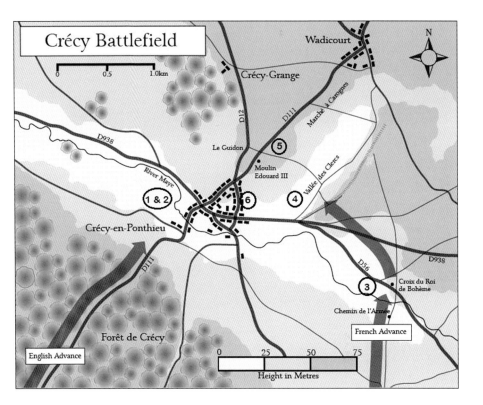

have been buried, and 9km to the south-east in Noyelles-en-Chaussée is the Chapelle de Trois Cents Morts, where 300 French knights were reported as having been interred. However, although the site described above has long been accepted as the most likely site of the battle, research published in 2015 suggests that the battle took place a little over 5km to the south of the traditional site, between Domvast and the Crécy forest.

The English army was probably deployed along the ridge facing generally south-east towards the Vallée des Clercs. This position gave them the advantage of holding the higher ground as the French approached along the Chemin de l'Armée. Approaching the English, the French would have had a significant obstacle between them and their enemy. Running along the eastern side of the Vallée des Clercs is a steep bank, probably associated with terracing of fields for agricultural purposes, with a slope in excess of 45 degrees, rising as high as 6m in places and averaging more than 2m in height along its length. Similar obstacles can be found in modern equestrian eventing, but for large numbers of armoured horsemen, crossing the ground at speed, descending this bank could only have resulted in chaos and disaster. Thus, even allowing for the rather precipitate attack of the French, it is more likely that the embankment served to channel the French along the face of the English army before they turned to face the English, having entered the valley from the south-west near the junction of the modern D56 and D938.

Preliminaries and the Advance to the Battlefield

The French set out from Abbeville on Saturday, 26 August, initially towards Noyelles-sur-Mer, close to the ford of Blanchetaque. They were confident that King Edward would flee in face of the risk of combat with a numerically greatly superior French army, and the King of Bohemia was mocked when he expressed the view that the English would stand and fight. Then news came that Edward was indeed stationary at Crécy, and Philip changed direction. The line of advance of Philip's army was north, skirting to the east of the Crécy forest, and traditionally along the axis of a track, now known as the Chemin de l'Armée, running north past the site of the Croix du Roi de Bohême and across the D56 and D938.

The English army is estimated to have been about 14,000 strong, comprising 2,800 men-at-arms, 3,000 mounted archers and 8,000 infantry, of whom perhaps 5,000 were archers. It was formed into three divisions. King Edward made good use of the time before the anticipated arrival of the French to make careful preparations making use of the agricultural terracing and the slope overlooking the gentle bowl of the Vallée des Clercs. The nature of these preparations and the disposition of the English army are open to widely differing interpretations. An enclosure was formed with all the carts and carriages, with only one entrance, but the purpose of this laager is not certain. It may have been simply to protect the horses and baggage, but some accounts place greater importance on the laager and see it as a key element of the English deployment.

The most common interpretation of the battle has the three English divisions aligned one behind the other, with the enclosure to the rear. At first sight, this might seem to have left the English flanks exposed, with the army drawn up on a narrow front. However, the ground on the left flank of the assumed English position falls away into a reentrant which would have provided some, albeit modest, defence. This could have been reinforced with the skilful deployment of archers. In addition, Edward may well have judged that the French were incapable of exercising sufficiently effective command and control to carry out an attack on his flanks and that, in any case, their overconfidence, spirit of élan and indiscipline would inevitably result in a frontal attack where defence in depth would offer the English a distinct advantage.

The vanguard under the command of the Prince of Wales, the Black Prince, and the Earls of Northampton and Warwick was in front. Behind the prince was the second division commanded by the Earls of Arundel, Suffolk and Huntingdon. In the rear was the king with the third division, with Edward III observing events from the vantage point of the windmill. The deployment of the archers has been the subject of much debate, centred on obscure descriptions in contemporary accounts, but the most probable disposition was that there were bodies of archers on either side of the divisions of men-at-arms, with some held in the rear to defend the baggage enclosure. It is also possible that there were initially archers in front of the army who could withdraw to the flanks as the French approached.

The alternative interpretation of the English deployment centres on the use of the laager as the key element of the defensive position. It has been calculated by Richard Barber that a circular formation constructed from a double row of carts with a circumference of around 650m, with a gap in the front about 100m wide, would have been possible with the estimated number of carts with the army. This would have provided an area sufficiently large to accommodate the men-at-arms and infantry. Deployment of the archers on both sides of the opening inside the laager and in cornfields and trees outside the opening would allow concentrated shooting on the French trying to penetrate the enclosure. It is possible that the artillery was deployed below carts on both sides of the opening. This deployment would fit as well with the terrain as the more conventional deployment does, with the added advantage of negating any weaknesses on the flanks due to the topography.

There are conflicting accounts of when the battle started, but it seems likely that the English were arrayed long before the battle, with the opportunity taken for a meal and for archers to dig pits to hamper the French cavalry. The king passed among the men giving words of encouragement. In mid-afternoon news was received that the French

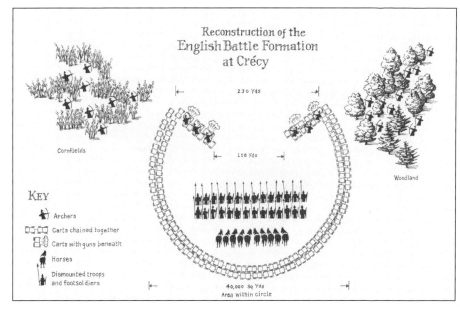

A reconstruction of the English battle formation. (Richard Barber)

were close by. Trumpets were sounded and the men armed and prepared for battle. It was traditional on the eve of battle for knighthoods to be bestowed, and Sir Alan la Zouche and Sir John de Lisle were elevated to the rank of banneret and a number of squires were knighted.

When Philip had received reports of the English presence at Crécy, he had sent four knights to reconnoitre the disposition of Edward's army. They reported that the English were drawn up in three divisions. As the French army moved inexorably forward towards the English, Philip took advice. The knight Henri le Moine advised that, since it was late in the day, they should wait overnight and make use of the time to organize the army for an attack on the English next morning. This was agreed, but unfortunately for Philip events were running ahead of the commanders and the sheer momentum of the advance meant that it was too late to prevent battle. The men in the front halted, but for reasons of honour those behind would not retire until those in front had done so. Others in the rear tried to advance, and in the resulting chaos some of the French came into contact with the English and battle could not now be delayed. The time was now late in the afternoon, possibly as late as 6.00 p.m.

The Battle

There is uncertainty about the organization of the French army, with varying accounts of between three and nine divisions. It is more probable that there were just three divisions, which was a conventional pattern in the Middle Ages. In addition, there was a contingent of mercenary Genoese crossbowmen under the command of Carlo Grimaldi and Anton Doria. The strength of the French army is uncertain, but it has been estimated that there were between 10,000 and 12,000 men-at-arms, with a large but unquantified number of common infantry and several thousand Genoese crossbowmen.

It was the Genoese who bore the brunt of the opening phase of combat. Grimaldi and Doria ordered their men to advance. They did so in three stages, shouting loudly on each occasion. The crossbowmen were at a disadvantage: they did not have their *pavises* – shields behind which they would normally shelter while loading their weapons – and much of their ammunition had not yet been unloaded from the wagons. The crossbow was an effective weapon, but it suffered from a slower rate of shooting than the English longbow. The problems of the crossbowmen appear to have been compounded by rainfall before the battle. This was said to have soaked the strings of the bows, rendering them unusable. If this were the case, then presumably it would have had a similar effect on the longbows. A perhaps more credible report indicates that the problem caused for the Genoese by the rain was not related to soaked bowstrings, but to the difficulty of gaining sufficient purchase in slippery conditions to secure the stirrup of the bow so that the string could be drawn.

The English archers initially remained motionless. They then stepped forward and began to shoot. The impact on the unprotected Genoese and the first of the French cavalry was disastrous, with crossbowmen turning to flee, maddened horses crashing into the men on foot, and some French cavalry, provoked by what they saw as the cowardice of the Genoese, riding down and killing the crossbowmen. To add to the confusion of battle, the English may also have been firing cannon into the French ranks. Not only were the Genoese fleeing, but also many of the French were in disarray and leaving the field before they had even formed up.

There are, again, varying accounts of subsequent events. It has been suggested that the first two English divisions advanced to attack and

An artist's impression of Louis de Nevers, Count of Flanders, with a serjeant in his service. The count is wearing armour in the German style. The armour is typical of that worn by both sides, before complete sets of plate armour came into use. A bascinet with a 'Klapvisier' visor is worn over a mail coiffe or cap with the mail aventail also forming protection for the throat. Steel plate is worn on the chest, over mail and a padded jacket, and on the legs. The mail provides protection for the vulnerable armpits and groin not covered by plate armour. The saddle is made of wood covered in leather and sits high on the horse, giving the rider a stable position and lifting much of his weight away from the horse's spine. (Paul Hitchen)

rout the first two French divisions. According to this account, King Philip then drove the English back to the enclosure of carts, with Edward coming from behind the enclosure to attack Philip in the flank and rear and securing victory. Another version of events is that the French made as many as fifteen successive assaults on the English positions. These attacks were mainly mounted, although some, including the Count of Blois who lost his life, chose to dismount. The first version implies that the English, having chosen and prepared a strong defensive position, and fighting dismounted as was common practice for the armies of Edward III, abandoned the high ground to attack the French at an early stage of the battle. It is difficult to see why they should have done so, and the second account with the English holding their ground in the face of French attacks is more probable, particularly if they were arrayed within the laager of carts.

At some point in the fighting it is said that the French broke into the Black Prince's division and a knight, named as Sir Thomas Norwich, was sent to King Edward in his windmill imploring him to send support since the Earl of Warwick and others with the prince feared that if the French numbers increased they would be unable to hold them off and the king's son would be in grave danger. The king is said to have refused, determined that the prince should win his spurs and that if the English were to carry the day the honour should go to him. Whether this tale is true or not, there is no doubt that the prince's division bore the brunt of the fighting and that the Black Prince acquitted himself well, with reports that he was twice brought to his knees by the ferocity of the fighting.

One account of the battle describes an incident, apparently not associated with Edward's reported refusal to come to the aid of the prince, when a gap was opened to the rear of the laager of carts and the rear-guard sallied forth to make a circling manoeuvre to come to the aid of the vanguard. This seems a plausible tactic, and is reminiscent of a decisive move made by the Black Prince at Poitiers ten years later. As the outcome of the battle became clear, King Philip finally left the field. Rather than returning to Abbeville as might have been expected, he made off north-eastwards to the castle of Labroye. Here he rested and ate and then rode through the night to Amiens with his escorts.

The battle abounds with stories of courage and chivalry. The death of the blind King of Bohemia, Jean de Luxembourg, is the most famous. He is said to have asked two knights to lead him into the mêlée, and the three rode to their deaths with their horses lashed together. It has been said that, as a tribute to the courage of the King of Bohemia, the Prince of Wales adopted the ostrich feather carried above the king's helmet and displayed it on his arms of peace which he wore in tournaments. These feathers still feature on the heraldic emblem of the Prince of Wales, although it may be that their origin is more prosaic and that they came from his mother's family. The Count of Alençon's standard-bearer refused to put his helmet on until he was good and ready, saying that once he had done so he would not take it off again. He was correct, being killed in the ensuing combat. King Philip VI fought bravely himself, having two horses killed under him, and suffering several wounds in hand-to-hand combat. There was a clear danger that he would be captured and he was led from the battle by the Count of Hainault. The *oriflamme*, the French war banner, which signified that no quarter would be given, was carried only when the king was present. At Crécy its bearer, Mile de Noyers, wrapped himself in the banner to prevent its capture, but it went down in the fighting and it was ripped to shreds and destroyed. The French king's standard was also brought low and the bearer was killed. It was not only French banners and standards that suffered in the fierce fighting. At one point the Black Prince's banner was in danger of capture. Richard Fitzsimon laid it down and stood over it while he fought to defend the prince. Fitzsimon and Thomas Daniel, who raised the banner again, were well rewarded by the Black Prince after the battle.

Casualties

The fighting had been ferocious, and French losses were heavy. Much as was the case at Agincourt in 1415, many men seem to have been crushed and died from suffocation as men-at-arms pressed forward onto those in front. Many notables were among those killed on the French side: they included the king's younger brother the Count of Alençon, Jean de Luxembourg, King of Bohemia, the King of Majorca, the Duke of Lorraine, the Archbishop of Sens, the Bishop of Noyon, and the Counts of Blois and Harcourt. The commanders of the Genoese crossbowmen, Carlo Grimaldi and Anton Doria, were also among the many dead named in chronicles and letters. Godefroy d'Harcourt is said to have attempted to protect his brother and nephew fighting for the French, but both were killed. He seems to have been profoundly affected by the fighting and before the year was out he had abandoned the English cause and transferred his allegiance to Philip once again.

Overall casualty figures are unknown, and, as was frequently the case in the Middle Ages, round figures of casualties, often greatly exaggerated, were common in written accounts. At one end of the scale one writer gave an extraordinarily precise figure of 1,542 French men-at-arms killed. It was by no means unusual in the medieval period to discount those of lower rank, and the writer made no attempt to quantify the number of infantry killed. At the other end of the scale one chronicler put French losses at 12,000 knights with up to 16,000 commoners. The same chronicler put English killed at 300 knights. What is beyond doubt is that French losses were much larger than those of the English.

The French king had ordered that the *oriflamme* should be raised, signifying that no quarter should be given, to prevent his men being distracted from the fighting in the search for valuable prisoners. In response King Edward raised the Dragon standard, which had a similar meaning to the *oriflamme*. The result of these actions was a higher death rate than might otherwise have been the case, with no prisoners recorded as having been taken on the day of the battle.

The Aftermath

There was no immediate pursuit of the French as the battle came to a close. It would have been late in the day and the men would have been exhausted. The English army was kept arrayed until near midnight when they were allowed to stand down but not to disarm. The king dined with the senior men in the army.

The next morning some of the English set out to see what was happening. Some French troops were still on the battlefield, possibly those of the Duke of Lorraine and the Count of Savoy who arrived the day after the battle, and made a stand. They were driven off by Thomas Beauchamp and William Bohun. In addition, it is said that there were large numbers of common French people who thought that the approaching troops were French. They paid dearly for their mistake with according to one report, probably much exaggerated, 4,000 being killed. Later Reginald de Cobham was sent out with a herald to identify the dead from their coats of arms and to draw up a list of French casualties. King Edward was concerned that the surviving French would regroup and return to the attack, and he kept his army on the battlefield throughout the day. Armour and equipment discarded on the battlefield were gathered together on the king's orders and burnt to prevent their future use. The scale of their victory appears to have shocked the English and there was no general celebration. Indeed, the death of the King of Bohemia was mourned in a service conducted by the Bishop of Durham.

A great victory had been achieved but King Edward could not rest on his laurels. The French king was alive and had not been captured and considerable numbers of the French remained at large despite the heavy casualties. However, the king already had his next objective in his sights, and on Monday, 28 August, the English set out on the march towards Calais. The news of the great victory quickly reached England and two royal councillors who had fought at the battle, Bartholomew Burghersh and John Darcy, reported to a council of bishops at Westminster and explained the king's plans to besiege and take Calais. On 6 September writs were sent out to the principal English towns to announce the victory and to call upon merchants to bring supplies and munitions for the siege of Calais.

What was the Impact of the English Victory?
The victory at Crécy was far from being decisive. Edward had not brought France to the brink of collapse as his son the Black Prince was to do with his victory at Poitiers ten years later. The French king remained at liberty and he still had at his disposal considerable resources in men and wealth. However, the English defeat of a powerful French army sent shock waves across Europe. Furthermore, the position of Edward at home was strengthened greatly by his success, and he could now more easily raise taxes through Parliament to pursue the war. He was, therefore, able to deploy and sustain the considerable force required to besiege Calais for almost a year before its eventual capture. A truce followed and within two years the Black Death swept across Europe. When war returned in 1355 the English ascendancy continued, due in no small part to the impact of the English successes at Crécy and Calais on both the French and the English.

Why were the English Victorious?

The English victory against superior numbers on foreign soil was a remarkable achievement which meant that they were now recognized as a force to be reckoned with. There are many factors which contributed to their success. Many of the men and their leaders were experienced in Edward's wars with Scotland and in earlier campaigns in the Hundred Years War. In addition, they had been together already for six weeks since landing in France. They might sometimes disregard discipline on the march when there was the prospect of plunder, but they were disciplined on the battlefield. In contrast, the French army, although it also had experienced men and commanders, was assembling as the English marched through France, and suffered from poor discipline.

The longbow was undoubtedly a key factor in the battle, particularly in the initial stages when the archers routed the Genoese crossbowmen and then broke the ranks of the cavalry before they made contact with the English men-at-arms. However, the archers could not win the battle alone and as the fighting progressed, defeat or victory turned on the outcome of the hand-to-hand combat between the men-at-arms. Although it has been a matter of controversy, there is little doubt that artillery was used at the battle, probably multi-barrelled guns mounted on carts and firing lead shot. No doubt they added noise and smoke to the chaos of battle, but they would have had a very slow rate of fire and are unlikely to have had much impact on the outcome of the fighting. They may have been used to defend the laager of wagons, rather than for direct fire in the main combat.

Morale always plays an important part in fighting efficiency, and never more so than when hand-to-hand combat is involved. It is likely that English morale was high. Even though faced by greater numbers, they would have had a justified self-belief based on a successful campaign to date, notably with the sack of Caen. They had been together for many weeks and knew each other, and also they were in a good defensive position. The French army, in contrast, had been hastily assembled and lacked coherence. The French knew of the widespread damage inflicted in Normandy which King Philip had been powerless to stop. Furthermore, they had seen the French king's challenge to the English to do battle outside Paris come to nothing. Nevertheless, we cannot assume that the French morale was low. They

An artist's impression of an English archer wearing the livery of the Earl of Oxford. Archers would wear a range of protection. If they were fortunate this could include mail, but more often than not they would rely on some form of padded and reinforced jacket. Those who had protective headgear might wear steel helmets, including bascinets, or hats made of boiled leather over a wickerwork frame reinforced by steel strips. Archers would also carry weapons in addition to their bows, often a dagger, a sword or an axe. (Paul Hitchen)

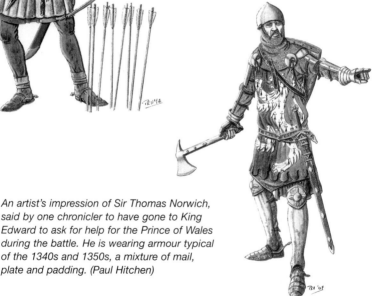

An artist's impression of Sir Thomas Norwich, said by one chronicler to have gone to King Edward to ask for help for the Prince of Wales during the battle. He is wearing armour typical of the 1340s and 1350s, a mixture of mail, plate and padding. (Paul Hitchen)

clearly fought with great courage and displayed arrogance and great self-confidence, even if this proved to be misplaced.

Perhaps the most important factor was a strong tactical doctrine which had been tried and tested by Edward III in his wars with the Scots. Contrary to the French practice of relying on mounted men-at-arms, coupled with disdain approaching scorn for the common foot-soldier and professional crossbowmen, the English placed the emphasis on what would now be known as a combined arms concept. This brought together three key elements: a strong defensive position, the employment of archers to disrupt the enemy approach to contact, and the use of dismounted men-at-arms in hand-to-hand combat once contact had been made.

The English and French Armies of the Hundred Years War
Raising and Maintaining Armies

Certain towns and castles would be garrisoned in times of peace, but in general the French and English kings did not maintain standing armies during the Hundred Years War. Instead, armies were raised for specific purposes or periods. The English armies were notable for the widespread use of the system of indenture for their recruitment and administration. Indentures were contracts between the king and his subordinate captains. They were so called because they were written in duplicate on a parchment which was then cut into two pieces along a toothed or indented line. In the case of dispute, the two pieces could be matched to establish their authenticity. The indentures specified the size and composition of the company to be provided, with numbers of men-at-arms and archers. Pay, length and conditions of service, and terms for ransoms for prisoners and for the share of the spoils of war were also detailed.

In France at the start of the war and at the time of Crécy armies were recruited through a feudal levy (the *arrière-ban*), but after Crécy in 1346 and Poitiers in 1356 the system became discredited and Charles V introduced reforms. Armies during the French recovery from 1369 were composed of contracted volunteers commanded by captains appointed by the king much as in the English case. They were well disciplined, centrally controlled and effective. By the time of Agincourt in 1415 the political instability in France had undermined many of the reforms made by Charles V. Nevertheless, measures were put in place to raise taxes to fund troops supplied by the nobility and gentry, and royal officials such as the constable, marshal, admiral and master of the crossbowmen. During the latter stages of the Hundred Years War Charles VII prepared the way for an effective army to drive the English from France by re-establishing royal control of the army, designating commanders and providing the pay for the men.

Composition of the Armies

The English armies were generally home-grown, with men drawn from throughout England, Wales and Ireland. However, there were also sometimes contingents of Gascons drawn from the Duchy of Aquitaine, and soldiers of fortune from other areas are also found on muster rolls. Indeed, at Crécy there was a substantial number of German men-at-arms. Archers formed a high proportion of the men in English armies. The archers did not fight from horseback, but many were mounted for the march to increase their mobility. The ratio of archers to men-at-arms varied. At Crécy archers may have accounted for half the strength of the army. As the war progressed the trend was for a larger proportion to be archers, although at Poitiers ten years after Crécy they accounted for only about one-third of the Black Prince's Anglo-Gascon army. At Agincourt the proportion of archers was around four-

fifths. French armies made much greater use of mercenaries than did the English, such as the large number of specialist Genoese crossbowmen at Crécy, and they also drew on militia from the towns and local levies of limited military value. The French emphasis was on the man-at-arms rather than on *gens de trait* (which included both archers and crossbowmen).

Although Scotland was the *de facto* ally of France during the war, there were no Scots at Crécy. The direct involvement of the Scots increased as the war progressed. There were Scots men-at-arms in the

Artist's impression of a French infantryman in the colours of the Paris militia. (Paul Hitchen)

French army at Poitiers and substantial numbers of Scots fighting alongside the French in the latter stages of the war.

Tactics

The preferred English tactic in set-piece battles was for the men-at-arms to dismount and to fight on foot in a strong defensive position which optimized the effectiveness of the archers. The objective was to hold position and wait for the enemy to come to them. This worked well against the Scots in the years before the Hundred Years War and at Crécy. At Poitiers the French did not initially oblige and it was only when the Black Prince was seen to be disengaging that the French launched an ill-coordinated attack. At Agincourt Henry V advanced towards the French to provoke a French attack, but then held his position as the French responded and moved forward to meet the English.

At Crécy the French had pinned their hopes on an attack by their mounted men-at-arms and knights, but the archers inflicted heavy casualties and the French finally broke on the line of dismounted English men-at-arms. However, French commanders were not slow to learn lessons from the impact of the archers at Crécy. At both Poitiers and Agincourt they adapted their tactics by fighting with the majority of their men on foot with small squadrons of heavily armed cavalry used to attempt to neutralize the English archers. In both cases poor execution of the plan rendered these tactics ineffective and the main bodies of French men-at-arms were still exposed to the shooting of the archers before they could come into hand-to-hand contact with the English.

The Longbow

The longbow used by archers in the armies of the English kings during the Hundred Years War was a formidable weapon. The bow was made of yew, imported ideally from the mountainous regions of Spain or Italy, and about 1.8m long. The natural characteristics of the wood – the resistance to compression of the heart wood used inside the stave, and the resistance to tension of the sap wood on the back – meant that great strength was required to draw the bow. Draw weights of 64kg may have been typical, with some thought to have been more than 80kg. For comparison, a modern sport longbow has a draw weight of between 13 and 27kg. Arrows typically weighed 113g, more than five times the weight of a modern competition arrow. Ranges of well in excess of 240m have been achieved with replica bows. One of the strengths of the longbow was its greater rate of shooting than that of the crossbow. It has been suggested that an archer could shoot up to twelve arrows per minute, compared to a crossbowman shooting two bolts per minute. One chronicler of the Battle of Crécy commented that the English archers could fire at three times the rate of a crossbowman, and this suggests that a more realistic sustained rate of shooting might be closer to five or six arrows per minute. There is much debate over the effectiveness of the longbow. By the late fifteenth century high-quality plate armour provided increasingly effective protection against arrows, but at the time of Crécy armour was less well developed and mainly comprised mail overlaid with plates rather than articulated suits of plate armour. That the longbow remained in service well into the sixteenth century, as witnessed by the finds on Henry VIII's *Mary Rose* which sank in 1545, is testimony in itself to the effectiveness of the weapon. In addition, even where armour was not penetrated, the impact of just one arrow delivered with the force of such bows would have been considerable. Archers could shoot with great accuracy, and it was exceedingly dangerous for a man-at-arms to raise his visor. The future Henry V had discovered this to his cost when shot in the face at the Battle of Shrewsbury in 1403. It seems that King Philip may also have suffered an arrow wound in the face at Crécy.

An artist's impression of a crossbowman with his pavise. (Paul Hitchen)

David Pim and Chris Dawson of the English Warbow Society with replica longbows of around 55kg and 50kg draw weight at full draw. (Peter Hoskins)

Steel armour-piercing arrow head. (Chris Dawson)

The medieval crossbow had a long history with progressive improvements made over the centuries. By the fourteenth century steel bows were in use, sometimes lashed to the stock with cord. Later bows had a range of mechanical aids for drawing the string, which allowed higher draw weights. At the time of Crécy, however, three simple methods were predominant: placing the feet on the bow and pulling the string with the hands; placing the string in a hook on a waist belt and driving the bow away with a foot in a stirrup below the bow; and a similar system with two hooks for stronger bows. Earlier crossbows had a similar range to the longbow, and as stronger bows were made to take advantage of mechanical means of drawing the string, so ranges increased to around 360m. The crossbow was an effective weapon. It had the advantage that it could be held in a cocked condition which enabled more deliberate aiming. However, its disadvantage compared to the longbow was its slow rate of shooting – around two bolts per minute. While drawing the bow, the crossbowman was vulnerable and in need of protection by a shield or *pavise*. Its steel bow also made it a heavy weapon to hold and to handle.

The Battlefield by Car, on Foot or by Bike

The tour starts in the centre of Crécy-en-Ponthieu with the church and the museum. It then takes the visitor to view the battlefield from the French approach and then from the position thought to have been occupied by the English army.

There are several places where refreshments can be found. The Café du Commerce, 40 Rue du Maréchal Leclerc de Hauteclocque (GPS 50.252079, 1.881243), +33 (0) 3 22 23 50 59, serves snacks throughout the day and the proprietor was particularly obliging when I visited, allowing me to leave my back-pack there while I toured the battlefield.

Visiting the Battlefield by Car

Start with a look at the church of St Severin (Point 1) and a visit to the museum (Point 2). Then leave Crécy on the D938 towards Arras and fork right onto the D56 on leaving the village. The Croix du Roi de Bohême (Point 3) is 1.5km from the junction of the D938 and D56. The only parking is on the side of this quite busy road. The Chemin de l'Armée, a grass track, crosses the road near the cross. Return towards Crécy, and at the junction with the D938 turn right and park near the pizza restaurant on the side of the road. A short walk, about 300m, along a track off to the left beside a wood on the left leads into the Vallée des Clercs (Point 4) with the embankment rising on the right and reaching 2m in height by the end of the wood. From this position there is a clear view of the viewing platform 1km to the north-west, close to where the windmill used by King Edward is thought to have stood, with the English positions below. Return to the car and follow the D938 back into Crécy. Turn right after 800m onto the D12 and after a further 400m turn right onto the D111. After 300m there is parking and access to the viewing platform (Point 5) with panoramic views of the battlefield. Return to the village on the D111 to the monument to Jean de Luxembourg (Point 6) to complete the tour.

Visiting the Battlefield on Foot or by Bike
The tour distance on foot is 6.25km. As with the tour by car, start with a look at the church of St-Severin (Point 1) and a visit to the museum (Point 2). Then leave Crécy on the D938 towards Arras and fork right onto the D56 on leaving the village. The Croix du Roi de Bohême (Point 3) is 1.5km from the junction of the D938 and D56. The Chemin de l'Armée, a grass track, crosses the road near the cross. Turn left to follow the track. After 300m, at the intersection with a further track, the surface is composed of stone and packed earth; continue straight on and turn left on reaching the D938 after a further 300m. Just before a pizza restaurant on the right-hand side of the road, immediately before the junction of the D938 and the D56, turn right onto a packed-earth and stone track leaving a wood on the left. This track leads into the Vallée des Clercs (Point 4). The embankment starts to rise on the right-hand side of the track and by the end of the wood is 2m high. At the end of the wood turn left, and the viewing platform, with the English position just below, comes into view. Turn right once again at the northern corner of the wood and then take the first track on the left to climb the hill to the D111. Turn left and follow the road to the viewing platform (Point 5), which gives a panoramic view of the battlefield. From the viewing platform follow the D111 into the village. Turn left to follow the D12, the Rue du Général de Gaulle, and then right once again onto the D111, the Place du Huit Mai 1945 and then Rue du Huit Mai 1945, and left into the Place Jean de Luxembourg with the monument to Jean de Luxembourg (Point 6).

The first 300m of track from the Croix du Roi de Bohême is on a grass surface. An alternative route for cyclists is to take the D56 back towards the village from the cross and take the track to the right after 300m to rejoin the walking route. The final 330m of the track to the D938 is on a stone and earth surface. The tracks along the Vallée des Clercs and up to the D111 near the viewing platform have a similar natural surface. If cyclists wish to avoid these tracks they should follow the route by car.

What to See
Recommended Viewing Points in Crécy and on the Battlefield
Point 1: The church of St-Severin, Rue de l'Église (GPS 50.252663, 1.899096), is mainly of fifteenth- and sixteenth-century construction. It did not play a part in the battle but the clock-tower surmounted by a

Church of St-Severin, Crécy. (Peter Hoskins)

watch platform is thought to be contemporary with the battle. An observer positioned there would have been well placed to see the approach of the English from the forest in the south-west and the French from the south-east.

Point 2: The museum in Crécy, La Musée de Crécy-en-Ponthieu, is at 4 Rue d'Écoles (GPS 50.251560, 1.881752), musée-crecyenponthieu.fr, +33 (0)3 22 31 33 13. It has a range of displays of equipment and weapons, tells the history of the battle, and caters for guided visits. It is open from early February to late November from Wednesday to Sunday between 10.00 and 12.15 and 14.15 and 18.00. Outside these periods guided visits can be arranged for groups of four or more people.

Point 3: The Croix du Roi de Bohême, 2km south-east of the village on the D56 (GPS 50.243807, 1.910731), commemorates the death of Jean de Luxembourg, King of Bohemia, of wounds sustained in the battle. The site of the cross is traditionally where the king died after the battle, although it is also claimed that he died later in the abbey of Valloires (*see* Tour Five, p. 167). The cross stands where the Chemin de l'Armée, the traditional route used by the French army approaching the battlefield, crosses the D56.

Croix du Roi de Bohême. (Peter Hoskins)

Point 4: The Vallée des Clercs (GPS 50.252663, 1.899096) is named after the clerks from Crécy Grange who are said to have passed along the valley identifying the French dead after the battle. Its significance for the battle is the influence of the embankment along its length on the south-eastern side on the advance of the French cavalry. At its south-western end it is about 2m high, but it is higher further to the north-east, reaching 6m in places. Looking to the north-west from the valley, with his back to the bank, the observer has a clear view of the English position in front of the viewing platform 800m distant.

The embankment of the Vallée des Clercs. The height and formidable nature of the obstacle can be clearly seen. (Peter Hoskins)

Point 5: The viewing platform, just off the D111 north-west of the village (GPS 50.256234, 1.887208), stands on the traditional location of

The viewing platform on the traditional location of the windmill used by Edward III to command the English army. (Peter Hoskins)

the windmill where Edward III is said to have established his command post and directed the battle. The platform is a good vantage point to look out towards the battlefield stretching down from the hill to the Vallée des Clercs.

Point 6: The monument to Jean de Luxembourg, the blind King of Bohemia, in Place Jean de Luxembourg (GPS 50.252651, 1.882407) was

The monument to Jean de Luxembourg in Crécy-en-Ponthieu. (Peter Hoskins)

erected in 1905 to commemorate the king and his companions in arms who died at the battle.

Further Afield
Point 7: Three hundred French knights are said to have been buried at La Chapelle de Trois Cents Corps in Noyelles-en-Chaussée (GPS 50.204250, 2.004257).

Point 8: The church of the Nativity de la Vierge in Forest l'Abbaye (GPS 50.207377, 1.823913), a former Templar chapel, is traditionally believed to be an English burial site for those killed at the battle.

Point 9: The alternative battlefield site, proposed in 2015 by Michael Livingstone and Kelly de Vries in *The Battle of Crécy, A Casebook*, lies between the D928, which runs parallel to the south-eastern edge of Crécy forest, and the commune of Domvast. The proposed English position is on a triangular parcel of land bordered by the D928, the Chemin des Maillets and the Rue du Mont de Forêt (GPS 50.207858, 1.905251). The proposed position of the French army is centred on a five-way junction on the D12 to the north of Domvast (GPS 50.203048, 1.917493).

Maps

Maps at 1:25,000 and 1:100,000 scales
Published by the *Institut National de l'Information Géographique et Forestière (IGN)* www.ign.fr
Cartes de Randonnée – 1:25,000
2206O Crécy-en-Ponthieu
TOP 100 – 1:100,000
TOP100103 Amiens/Arras

How to Get There and Back by Public Transport

Beauvais, Lille and Paris airports are all practical for this tour. There is a main-line railway station at Abbeville and a bus service, run by Trans'80, Line 13, www.trans80.fr, between the railway station and Crécy-en-Ponthieu.

Where to Stay and Where to Eat

See www.crecyenponthieu.com and www.abbeville-tourisme.com for accommodation and refreshment.

FURTHER READING

There is a wide range of literature concerning the Battle of Crécy and the Hundred Years War. The suggestions that follow are based largely on the author's personal preference, and cover the Crécy campaign itself, the Hundred Years War in general, Agincourt and Poitiers, the other great battles of the war which live in English consciousness, and Edward III and the Black Prince.

Crécy
The Battle of Crécy, 1346, Andrew Ayton and Sir Philip Preston (Woodbridge, 2007)
The Road to Crécy, The English Invasion of France, 1346, Morgen Witzel and Marilyn Livingstone (Edinburgh, 2005)
The Chronicle of Geoffrey Le Baker of Swinbrook, Richard Barber, translated by David Preest (Woodbridge, 2012)
The Battle of Crécy: A Casebook, Michael Livingston and Kelly DeVries (Liverpool, 2015)

Agincourt
Agincourt 1415. A Tourist's Guide to the Campaign, Peter Hoskins with Anne Curry (Barnsley, 2014)
Agincourt, a New History, Anne Curry (Stroud, 2005; paperback edition, 2006)
Agincourt, the King, the Campaign, the Battle, Juliet Barker (London, 2005)
Azincourt, Bernard Cornwell (an historical novel), (London, 2009)
1415: Henry V's Year of Glory, Ian Mortimer (London, 2010)
The Agincourt Companion, A Guide to the Legendary Battle and Warfare in the Medieval World, Anne Curry, Peter Hoskins, Thom Richardson, and Dan Spencer (London, 2015)

The Hundred Years War
Trial by Battle, The Hundred Years War, Vol 1, Jonathan Sumption (London, 1999)

Trial by Fire, The Hundred Years War, Vol 2, Jonathan Sumption
(London, 2001)
Divided Houses, The Hundred Years War, Vol 3, Jonathan Sumption
(London, 2012)
Cursed Kings, The Hundred Years War, Vol 4, Jonathan Sumption
(London, 2015)
A fifth volume of Jonathan Sumption's history is expected in due
course.
The Agincourt War, Lt-Col. Alfred H. Burne (London, 1956; reprinted
Ware, 1999)
The Crécy War, Lt-Col. Alfred H. Burne (London, 1956; reprinted
Ware, 1999)

Poitiers
In the Steps of the Black Prince, the Road to Poitiers, 1355-1356, Peter
Hoskins (Woodbridge, 2011; paperback and kindle editions,
Woodbridge, 2013)
The Battle of Poitiers, 1356, David Green (Stroud, 2002)

Edward III
Edward III and the Triumph of England, Richard Barber (London, 2013;
paperback edition, London, 2014)
The Perfect King: The Life of Edward III, Father of the English Nation, Ian
Mortimer (London, 2008)
Edward III, W. Mark Ormrod (Yale, 2013)

The Black Prince
Edward, Prince of Wales and Aquitaine: A Biography of the Black Prince,
Richard Barber (Woodbridge, 2003)

INDEX

Since Edward III, king of England, Philip VI, king of France and Crécy are mentioned frequently throughout the text, they are excluded from this index of people and places. Illustrations are indexed in **bold** type.

Thiberville, 88
Torigny-sur-Vire, 51, 59, 73
Touraine, 36
Tournai, 28
Trastámara, Henry of, 32
Troarn, 86, **87**, 90, 91, 93, **94**
Troissereux, 130, 131, 138, 140
Troyes, Treaty of (1420), 38

Valloires, 160, 162, 163, 167, 172
Valognes, 46, 52, 59, 61
Valois, Catherine de, 35
Vendes, 52
Verdun, Raoul de, 48
Vernon, 89, 103, 104, 105, **106**,
    107, 110, 111, 118, **118–19**

Vessencourt, 130, 139

Wadicourt, 158, 159
Wallingford, 55
Warignies, Robert de, 53
Warwick, Earl of, 43, 45, 46, 54,
    107, 132, 133, 135, 156, 175,
    179
William I, King of England, 18,
    52, 85, 93
Wimille, 160, 161, 162
Wissant, 161, **161**, 162, 166

Zouche, Sir Alan la, 176